YOUR MONEY
OR
YOUR LIFE

YOUR MONEY
OR
YOUR LIFE

STRONG MEDICINE FOR
AMERICA'S HEALTH CARE SYSTEM

DAVID M. CUTLER

OXFORD
UNIVERSITY PRESS

OXFORD

UNIVERSITY PRESS

OXFORD   NEW YORK

AUCKLAND   BANGKOK   BUENOS AIRES   CAPE TOWN   CHENNAI
DAR ES SALAAM   DELHI   HONG KONG   ISTANBUL   KARACHI   KOLKATA
KUALA LUMPUR   MADRID   MELBOURNE   MEXICO CITY   MUMBAI   NAIROBI
SÃO PAULO   SHANGHAI   TAIPEI   TOKYO   TORONTO

First published by Oxford University Press, Inc., 2004
198 Madison Avenue, New York, New York 10016

www.oup.com

First issued as an Oxford University Press paperback, 2005
ISBN-13 978-0-19-518132-6

Oxford is a registered trademark of Oxford University Press

The Library of Congress has cataloged the cloth edition as follows:
Cutler, David M.
Your money or your life : strong medicine for America's health care system
/ David M. Cutler.
p. cm.
Includes bibliographical references and index.
ISBN-13 978-0-19-516042-0

1. Medical care—United States.
2. Health planning—United States.
3. Health behavior—United States.
4. Social medicine—United States.
I. Title.

RA395.A3C956 2004
362.1'0973—dc21   2003050673

5 7 9 8 6 4

Printed in the United States of America
on acid-free paper

To Gordon and Iris

and their

continued good health

Contents

Introduction:
Crisis by Design

The problems of medical care confront us daily: a bureaucracy that makes obtaining care difficult; doctors who are frustrated by insurance restrictions; more than 40 million people without health insurance. "Medical care is in crisis," we are repeatedly told, and so it is. Barely one in five Americans thinks the medical system works well.[1]

For all the talk about crisis, however, health reform has proven painfully difficult. President Bill Clinton proposed major health reform in 1992. It was defeated, largely as a result of the complexity of the changes. The Republican Congress attempted an overhaul of Medicare and Medicaid in 1995. Nothing came of it. Managed care regulation dies, universal coverage flounders, and cost containment sputters. In spite of good intentions, we accomplish far less in medical care than we should.

The political system certainly makes reform hard by fractionalizing control between the political parties and among various committees in Congress. Many powerful interests are also in favor of the status quo. But politics is not the whole story. There is a basic confusion about what kind of health care reform would improve the system. Consider the number of people who simultaneously believe that medical spending is too high but managed care limitations on spending are too stringent, who believe that doctors as a whole make mistakes but their own doctor does not, and who think that the United States has the worst medical care system in the world—unless you are sick. We hold seemingly contradictory views about basic health issues. Is it any wonder that we have difficulty agreeing on appropriate reforms?

The first task of a doctor is to note the patient's symptoms, and so it is with us. What is it about health care that is so troubling? *Cost* is the first issue; medical care is very expensive. The average person in the United States uses nearly $5,000 in medical resources each year. That is more than the total spent on automobiles, TVs, and computers combined. As a country, we spend more on health than the Chinese spend on everything, including all the tea in China. Who has not read of families priced out of insurance, of elderly people forced to choose between prescription medications and food, of telethons to raise funds for a sick child needing a transplant? Direct spending is but the tip of the iceberg. Insurance companies and governments spend four times what families do on medical care.

Cost increases are widely seen as problematic. "Rising Health Costs Signal Ominous Emerging Trend," *USA Today* recently warned.[2] Rising costs are an "ominous warning for the rest of the nation," according to the *Washington Post*,[3] and a "dangerous omen for all employers and all consumers," according to one expert.[4]

Access to health care is also a significant concern. More than 40 million people are uninsured. Not surprisingly, uninsured people get less care than insured people. The prestigious Institute of Medicine, an official advisory body for the federal government, estimates that 20,000 people die each year because they are uninsured—about as many deaths as among infants.[5] Lack of insurance bothers us for moral as well as medical reasons. In a country as rich as ours, it is difficult to accept that not everyone has health insurance. Other countries insure everyone, and at lower cost. Why can't the United States do the same?

The difficulties the already uninsured face are troubling enough. The fear of becoming uninsured torments millions more. In the past decade and a half, the number of Americans without health insurance rose by more than ten million, despite the best economy in generations. One in five people is uninsured at some point in a year;

one in three is uninsured at some point in a three-year period. For many, access to health insurance is often in jeopardy.

The *quality* of medical care is yet another trouble spot. We like to think of America's medical system as the best in the world, but the headlines jolt us from that perception. How frequently do we read about physicians operating on the wrong body part or giving the wrong therapy to a patient? Beyond the headlines, patients get medications to which they are allergic, have key tests or exam results misplaced, and endure longer hospital stays because of preventable complications. One study estimates that 50,000 to 100,000 people die every year of medical mistakes in hospitals,[6] making hospital errors a leading cause of death.

Outright errors are only the tip of the quality-of-care iceberg; there are other failings as well. Some people get too much care. About one in ten people undergoing a major operation does not meet the clinical criteria for that operation. Some areas of the country spend twice what others do on medical care, with little difference in mortality or quality of life. We waste a lot of money on care that has little value. In other cases, people get too little care. There are many diseases that are readily treatable, but for which rates of successful treatment are low. Only one-quarter of people with hypertension have their blood pressure successfully controlled, despite a wealth of effective medications. Management of diabetes, high cholesterol, depression, and asthma is similarly poor. What we do not prevent, we wind up treating later, frequently at higher cost.

But the news is not all bad. We are enamored by what medicine can do for us. Many diseases that were once a death sentence are now treatable. The prognosis for AIDS patients was decidedly poorer a decade ago, but most AIDS sufferers can now live without fear of imminent death. Heart disease incapacitated people in the 1950s and 1960s; today, living with the disease frequently means little change in routine.

Let me pose a hypothetical question. In 1950 medical spending was about $500 per person (adjusted for inflation). Today, it is nearly $5,000. Suppose you were offered that $4,500 increase back, but in exchange you could only have medical care at the 1950s level— doctors trained at that level, hospitals with 1950s equipment, medications from around at that time, and so on? Would you accept the money? My suspicion is that most would not; we value the things that medicine can do for us more than $4,500. But does that mean that increases in medical costs are worth it?

Why is the medical system's performance so mixed? What could be done to make it better? Start with a basic observation: The goal of medical care is to improve our health. The system works well if it improves health sufficiently to justify its cost, and poorly if it does not. That seems obvious, but it has deep implications. Most significantly, it implies that controlling medical costs is not an important goal in itself. Lowering costs is good if we are overspending, but bad if we are getting valuable care. We need to ask whether we are getting enough for our money, or whether the money we put into medical care would be better used on food, shelter, or other items.

I'll explore this issue in some detail. The evidence shows clearly that spending more has been good; we get a lot more out of the medical system than we put in. Further, because so many people do not get care when they need it, we could spend more on those people with excellent results. We worry far too much about wasting money on medicine.

The issue in spending is not how much we put in, but making sure we get value for our dollar. Can we do better than we have done? The answer is yes. There are two ways we could improve. The first is to extend the benefits of medicine to everyone. Insuring the uninsured would increase medical spending but also improve health. The investment in universal coverage is worth it if the health improvements are significant enough to justify the costs. From the societal perspective, I show that this is the case: The health of the uninsured would improve by more than enough to justify the added spending. Of course, not everyone benefits from universal insurance coverage; some people have safe, secure insurance already. But providing universal coverage would benefit enough people to make it a very fruitful investment. I present a way to cover the uninsured that would be responsible and affordable.

The second way to improve health care is to increase the value we get for our spending. We must eliminate the errors in the system, limit the amount of excessive care, and provide more care when it is underprovided. There are a number of reasons for these failures. Care is overused because physicians believe certain treatments will work, even though the literature suggests otherwise. Some services are underused because the system is a hassle. Surgeons make mistakes because people are fallible and computer technology is not used frequently enough as a backup. Is there a common denominator here?

There is, and it has to do with reimbursement. Medical care providers are paid on the basis of what they do. When they provide intensive services, they are paid well. Providing less intensive services is reimbursed much less well. As a result, medical professionals tend to perform too many intensive surgeries, while failing to do important routine monitoring and follow-up. Reimbursing sophisticated care well is important, but paying for it is not a guarantee of better health. The way to get the system to focus on health is to make payments dependent as much on the effectiveness of the services provided as on the quantity and sophistication of services. I propose a system in which doctors would be paid more for meeting care guidelines such as appropriate use of mammograms, cholesterol screenings, and flu shots; in which hospitals with better surgical outcomes would earn more; and in which insurers that took care of people would be better off financially. Good care would earn more than poor care.

The idea of paying for performance is not new—who is not judged on the quality of their work? But it is new in medical care. The medical system has not focused to any significant extent on how well it does what it does. Moving toward a system that rewards this thinking will orient medicine to making sure we are healthy, not just "treated." I will discuss why other proposals, such as the single-payer insurance model used in Canada or increased access to litigation in cases of harm would not accomplish these goals.

Making these changes will require concerted actions by the public and private sectors. Government is the only institution that can guarantee universal insurance coverage; the private sector has repeatedly failed at this task. At the same time, both the public and private sectors will need to overhaul their payment systems to encourage greater performance. Government and private insurers each pay for about 40 percent of medical spending (the rest is paid out of pocket by patients). No health reform will be successful without coordinated action from both sectors.

My interest in these topics came in a roundabout way. In 1993 I was in Washington, D.C., working on the Clinton administration's health reform effort. Remember the secret group of five hundred people out to reform the health care system? I was one of them. The Clinton plan was ultimately unsuccessful, but the experience lingered with me. I came back to my research full of questions. Why did the Clinton plan fail? I didn't really know. What should have been done differently? Almost everything. Did the premise of the plan even make sense? The last question particularly intrigued me (not least because I couldn't answer the first two). For the past decade, I have been researching and thinking about health care. What goes right and wrong? What drives the need for reform, and why is reform so difficult? This book is the result.

Economics is a technical subject, and the economics of medical care is complex indeed. Thus, there is a great deal of analysis behind many of the statements I make that, fortunately for the general reader, I will not detail here. For those interested, a technical appendix backing up the analytical conclusions is available on the Internet (http://post.economics.harvard.edu/faculty/dcutler/dcutler. html). Notes at the end of the book refer the interested reader to specific studies and provide a bit more commentary.

If the analysis is complex, though, the end product is straightforward. Money matters in health care as it does in few other industries. Where we have spent a lot, we have received a lot in return. Too often, however, we provide the wrong incentives or do not pay enough. By fixing these problems, we can make the medical system work better.

Your Money
or
Your Life

THE HEALTH
OF THE NATION:
A HISTORY

Before we consider the health care system, we need to agree on what we mean by health. Health is a slippery term—an idea easy to perceive but difficult to define. Good health enables us to live a vigorous and happy life. But what that involves changes over time. When life was spent being chased by saber-toothed tigers, good health meant being able to run and hide. Today, it may involve a positive feeling of self and the ability to use a computer keyboard. These multiple dimensions of health make health measurement difficult.

The easiest part of health to measure is length of life. A population that lives longer is healthier than one that does not live as long. Mortality has declined steadily in the United States since 1900—and likely since at least 1800.[1] The decline in mortality has been continuous, except for a decade or so beginning in the mid-1950s (a period I will discuss shortly).

A more natural metric of health than mortality is life expectancy, the average number of years that a person can expect to live. Given the mortality rates prevailing at the time, the typical baby born in 1900 could expect to live to about age 45.[2] Today, life expectancy is closer to 80, a dramatic improvement by any standard.

The overall trend toward longer life masks important changes in the source of longer life.[3] From 1800 until about 1940, reduced mortality was almost entirely the product of reduced infant and child mortality. In 1900, one in five infants died before age ten. By the mid-twentieth century, infant and child death was less than half as common. By contrast, life expectancy for those who survived the early years of life increased only slightly in this period.

The tragedy of high infant and child mortality around 1900 was a subject of great concern. Late in the 1800s, a leading French physician lamented: "Is it not humiliating for our country and for our generation that, in spite of public and individual hygiene, the mortality among the newly born is such that one can say, without fear of contradiction, that an infant just born has less chance than a man of ninety of living a week, and than an octogenarian of living a year?"[4]

Infant and child mortality was so high because infectious disease was rampant. The young develop disease antibodies slowly; in combination with their poor nutrition, this makes them particularly susceptible to infection. In an era without effective treatment for infectious disease, these infections were frequently fatal. Over time, several factors combined to reduce infectious disease mortality (see table).[5] Public health improvements, including clean water, sewers, and pasteurized milk, reduced disease exposure. Personal health practices such as hand washing and proper food storage were important too. Combined with better nutrition from improved agricultural output, these improvements limited disease susceptibility and aided recovery. The net effect was a major reduction in infant and child mortality.

Between 1940 and 1960, there was a subtle but important shift in the nature of mortality reduction. Infectious disease mortality continued to decline, but formal medical care began to play a larger role. The development of sulfa drugs in the 1930s and penicillin in the 1940s were the most significant events in medicine. Antibiotics were wonder treatments for infections. By 1960, infectious disease mortality had been substantially eliminated. Antibiotics are valuable for both young and old, and so mortality fell among all age groups. In the mid-twentieth century, we saw the first real increase in life expectancy at older ages.

Observers noting these trends were impressed, but they were grim in their outlook for the future. With infectious disease largely conquered by 1960, the leading killers were cardiovascular disease, cancer, and chronic conditions of old age. There was no experience of

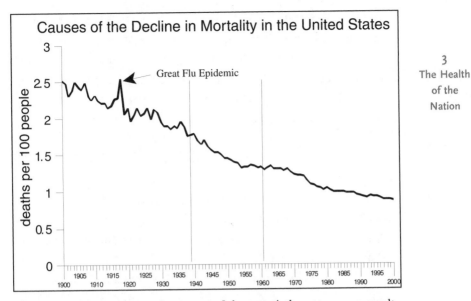

Causes of the Decline in Mortality in the United States

Great Flu Epidemic

Mortality has declined over the course of the twentieth century as a result of public health and nutritional improvements predominant in the period up to 1940, the development of antibiotics in the next two decades, and medical technology to treat cardiovascular disease and low-birth-weight infants especially since 1960. Mortality is age-adjusted. (United States Department of Health and Human Services, Centers for Disease Control and Prevention, National Center for Health Statistics)

improvement in any of these conditions. Famed biologist René Dubos expressed the pessimism well: "Modern medicine has little to offer for the prevention or treatment of chronic and degenerative diseases that dominate the pathological picture of technologic societies."[6] Sure enough, mortality rates in the United States stopped declining between the mid-1950s and the late 1960s.

But almost as soon as we began reconciling ourselves to a fixed life span, mortality rates once again started to fall rapidly. That decline continues. What observers in 1960 could not foresee was that chronic disease mortality could change. It could, and it did. Cardiovascular disease mortality led the way. Between 1960 and 2000 it declined as rapidly as infant and child mortality had earlier in the century. Since cardiovascular disease strikes mostly the middle-aged and elderly, mortality improvements since 1960 have increasingly affected older people.

At the other end of life, progress continues on infant mortality, which also fell after 1960. But here, too, the source of the declines is different from what it had been earlier in the century. Where declining infant mortality was formerly associated with reduced infectious disease, today it has much more to do with the survival of low-birth-weight infants. The neonatologist has replaced the hygienist as primary facilitator of infant survival.

Taken together, reduced mortality from cardiovascular disease and from medical advances in treating low-birth-weight infants represent a fundamental change in the nature of health improvements. Call it the medicalization of health. Formal medicine played almost no part in better health in 1900 and only a small part through 1950. Today, it is a major part.

We see this medicalization in the scale of our medical system. In 1950 medical spending was only $500 per person (in today's dollars), and medical care accounted for a mere 4 percent of gross domestic product (GDP). Today, we spend nearly $5,000 per person on medical care, and medical care accounts for almost 15 percent of GDP.

We also see it in the growing rigor of the system.[7] In 1900, doctors were poorly trained,[8] and infection was rampant, particularly in hospitals. In 1894 there were riots in Milwaukee when an ambulance came to take a child suspected of having smallpox to the hospital. The child had already lost one sibling in the institution, and his mother did not want to lose another. Facing 3,000 people armed with clubs, the ambulance attendants backed away.[9] The system had improved by 1950 but was still not great. Penicillin and sulfa drugs, along with basic sanitary measures, made hospitals a reasonable place to go when sick. Medical school training had improved.

But lack of knowledge was a major limiting factor. Physicians could see older people dying of heart attacks, and low-birth-weight infants dying of respiratory problems, but they did not know what to do. At the time, doctors were generalists. In 1950 there were very few medical specialties. There was a division between medicine and surgery, but little else.[10]

The lack of knowledge was the major factor limiting progress in healthcare. Vannevar Bush, director of the federal office of Scientific Research and Development in the 1940s, wrote a report for President

Franklin D. Roosevelt on the prospects for science after World War II.[11] Discussing medical research, Bush noted, "Notwithstanding great progress in prolonging the span of life and relief of suffering, much illness remains for which adequate means of prevention and cure are not yet known. While additional physicians, hospitals, and health programs are needed, their full usefulness cannot be attained unless we enlarge our knowledge of the human organism and the nature of disease. Any extension of medical facilities must be accompanied by an expanded program of medical training and research ... Further progress requires that the entire front of medicine and the underlying sciences of chemistry, physics, anatomy, biochemistry, physiology, pharmacology, bacteriology, pathology, parasitology, etc., be broadly developed."

Bush's report was instrumental in creating the National Science Foundation and the National Institutes of Health, which pioneered many of the medical innovations of the past half century. Better treatment of heart attack victims and low-birth-weight infants were some of the results. These institutions continue to promote medical advances today.

———————

Health involves quality as well as length of life. A population that lives long but is in poor health is not (much) better off than one with a shorter but healthier life span. Information about changes in quality of life is harder to obtain than information about changes in length of life, since quality of life is so much more difficult to measure. Still, we can see large improvements over time.

Physical health has improved immensely in the past few centuries. A prominent eighteenth-century physician described Italian workers thus: "Starvation and sickness are pictured on the face of the entire laboring class. You recognize it at first sight. And whoever has seen it will certainly not call any one of the people a free man ... Before sunrise, after having eaten a little and always the same unfermented bread that appeases his hunger only half-way, the farmer gets ready for hard work. With emaciated body under the hot rays of the sun he plows a soil that is not his and cultivates a vine that for him has no reward."[12] Even in 1800 a significant share of the European population did not have enough food even to wander around the city, let alone work under the demanding conditions of an industrialized workplace.[13]

By 1900 health had improved, though not to modern levels. In a 1905 speech at Johns Hopkins University, the great physician William Osler encouraged retirement at age 60, as people's capacity to do much that was constructive after that age was limited: "As it can be maintained that all the great advances have come from men under forty, so the history of the world shows that a very large proportion of the evils may be traced to the sexagenarians—nearly all the great mistakes politically and socially, all of the worst poems, most of the bad pictures, a majority of the bad novels, and not a few of the bad sermons and speeches."[14] Fortunately (from Osler's vantage point), people rarely lived to those ages.

Medical records show the poor quality of life of older persons a century ago. The best data we have on health early in the twentieth century is from medical examinations of Civil War veterans (young men in the mid-1860s), performed to determine their eligibility for federal pensions.[15] Respiratory disease was three times higher in Civil War veterans than it is among elderly people today. Cardiovascular disease was more prevalent as well, as were joint and back problems. Across the board, modern men are in substantially better health than men of a century ago.

Economic advance is one factor in this change. Manual labor was common around 1900. Manual laborers suffered significant joint and back problems; were exposed to dust, gases, and fumes (leading causes of respiratory disease); and encountered many more infectious diseases. The economic environment is much better than today's elderly experienced when they were working.

There has been more debate about health trends since 1950, the beginning of the era of big medicine. Some argue that medicine is sustaining people who have a very poor quality of life, for whom the benefits of a longer life are not very great. This phenomenon has been termed the "failure of success."

A significant amount of research has examined trends in quality of life in the past few decades to see if it has improved or worsened. Because health impairments are particularly concentrated at older ages, research has focused on the health of the older population. At the upper end, many more seniors are in extremely good health than used to be the case. My favorite statistic, because I myself race, is the age distribution of marathon runners. In 1980 about 5 percent of marathon runners were over the age of 50. Today, the share is double that.[16] This is true even though more people at all ages are running marathons; the elderly have taken up the sport at a greater rate than the young. Even if not running marathons, many more elderly engage in leisure activities such as tennis and golf than used to be the case. Active retirement is a recent and widespread innovation.[17]

The bottom end of the health distribution is, in many ways, more important than the top. Are there many more very sick people than there used to be? Some research analyzing data from the 1960s and 1970s, just at the start of the modern era of medical advance, suggested that quality of life was decreasing—there were increasing numbers of elderly with significant physical impairments.[18] More elderly were reporting themselves unable to work than did just a few years earlier, and diagnosis of chronic disease was much more common. Success did indeed seem to have failed.

But the measures of health employed in these studies were relatively poor. The federal disability program expanded during this time, so one would naturally expect more people to say they were unable to work. The increase in chronic disease might just as easily have resulted from increased diagnosis as from true increases in disease.[19] Some researchers looked at the evidence and concluded that the decrease in quality of life was largely illusory.[20] But in truth, nobody was really sure what was happening. Better data were needed.

Beginning in the early 1980s, efforts were made to collect such data. Researchers developed surveys that measured underlying physical functioning, not report of disease. People are asked about their ability to perform basic activities such as bathing, eating, and walking, and social tasks such as shopping, managing money, and doing light housework. Health surveys with these questions have been administered widely and consistently to large numbers of elderly people since the early 1980s.[21] We now have two decades of such studies, and the results are clear: the elderly are much healthier than they were two decades ago. There is no "failure of success"; rather, there are more victories.[22]

The change in disability has been large. One in four elderly people had difficulty living independently in the early 1980s. Today, there are fewer than one in five. The nursing home population today is virtually the same as two decades ago, despite a major increase in the elderly population. The health of the population is improving, even as more people live to older ages.

———————————

While physical impairment is relatively rare in the non-elderly population, many non-elderly contend with mental health problems. There have been concerns that the nation's mental health has suffered in the past few decades, even as our physical health has improved. Life has more stresses, families are less cohesive, and social ties are weaker than they used to be (at least in perception; good data are scarce), all possibly leading to worse mental health.

Data on the mental health of the population are difficult to obtain. Some surveys of mental illness were conducted in the 1950s and 1960s, but they often used particular samples of people that make them nonrepresentative of the United States as a whole (for example, residents of midtown Manhattan). And the definition of mental illness has changed over time. For example, homosexuality was considered a mental illness until 1973. Social phobia and post-traumatic stress disorder were first recognized in 1979. It is difficult to evaluate disease trends when the measures of disease change over time. As a result, the true state of the nation's mental health is not known. But it is safe to say that mental illness is more commonly diagnosed now than it used to be, and we are more aware of the enormous toll that mental illness takes on people. Spending on mental health care is also significantly higher. Because of the particular importance of this issue, I focus on mental health in chapter 4.[23]

———————————

Considering all this evidence, it is clear that there has been a revolution in human health dating back more than two centuries and continuing through today. We live longer and better lives than the people who lived before us. Until about 1950 the improvement in health was most significantly a result of improved nutrition, basic public health, and the introduction of effective medications. Infectious disease was the leading killer, and these changes substantially reduced its threat.

Since 1950 the modern medical system has been more important in extending life. A reduction in the number of cases of cardiovascular disease and infant death are most significant in contributing to longer life. Physical disability has decreased as well. In the post-1950 era, health improvements have more directly followed medical advances, as the medical system grew into its modern shape. This post-1950 era is the key period to consider in evaluating modern medicine, and it is on this period that I shall focus. Before doing so, we need to consider how to place a value on health improvements.

2

PRICING THE PRICELESS[1]

"HEALTH IS PRICELESS," THE OLD saying goes. "If you don't have your health, what do you have?" We are willing to do a lot for better health. We spend money on doctors, give up our favorite foods, devote hours to the gym, and seek out the latest medical advances, all in the name of better health.

The importance of health is uncontroversial. But resources are limited, and so we need a way to prioritize. Suppose that doctors invent a wonderful new surgery that will save the lives of some heart attack victims and improve quality of life for others—but the operation costs $10,000. Should we as a society pay for it, for example, by adding it to services paid for by Medicare or private insurance policies? Improving the health of cardiovascular disease sufferers is valuable, but money spent on heart attacks cannot be spent caring for low-birth-weight infants, buying additional textbooks, or cleaning up the environment. How are we to know if heart attack care is worth more than these other uses?

Currently, we do not make these decisions in any systematic way. All medical treatments that improve health are approved for use, generally at the doctor's discretion. As a result, we worry that we spend too much on medical care. In the United Kingdom and Canada, by contrast, limits are placed on what can be done. The government determines how many surgical facilities are available, and doctors can only operate on so many patients. Those judged the highest priority receive operations. Is this type of system better? Valuing health is an integral part of assessing this answer.

_____

Valuing health is among the most difficult of all topics to discuss in polite company. It involves ethical, legal, religious, political, and economic values. There is no way to do it that does not give us at least some discomfort. But we must confront it if we are to make these basic decisions.

Start with the central question: Whose value of health are we considering? Usually, we think about "what would I want if I got sick?" Differences by income are immediately apparent. Rich people are willing and able to pay more for a life-saving medical treatment than the poor. Should we use the value for the rich or the value for the poor (or perhaps a higher value for the rich than the poor)? But this personalized fashion is not right. The health advances we are valuing are not treatments for imminent injury, but rather treatments for potential injuries. How much is it worth now to get to live longer if one has a heart attack? How much is it worth to save a low-birth-weight baby, should one be born in the family? We don't know exactly what we will need; we know only that some will need it.

Consistent with this probabilistic framework, most of these advances are financed by insurance. The rich do not buy heart attack care when they are sick; they buy insurance when they are healthy that allows them access to care when they are sick. Everyone in the same insurance plan is in the same position when they get sick; money is not a (major) deciding factor. So, valuing health is equivalent to asking how much people value an insurance policy that provides access to new medical treatment.

Even in this setting, the rich may value health insurance more than the poor. At the same price, rich people will be more able to buy health insurance than the poor. In practice, though, many of the health advances realized by the poor have been paid for, directly or indirectly, by people with higher incomes. Many of the poor qualify for Medicaid, which is financed from general taxation. Poor people who are uninsured receive "free care"—care given without charging the recipient, but ultimately paid for by passing the costs along to the insured. In practice, then, the distinction between rich and poor is less consequential than it first seems. Throughout this discussion, therefore, I focus on the value of health for the typical person, not considering variations in income or other attributes.

Religion guides the views of many about life and health. The Bible records that Moses lived to age 120 in reasonably good health ("his eye was not dim, nor his natural force abated").[2] A common Jewish blessing is to wish this for others.

Philosophers have also proposed various criteria to value health, frequently differentiating between more and less valuable health. Ethicist Daniel Callahan has argued that health has a very high value up to the point of premature death—around age 65 or 70—but a lower value after that.[3] Others argue that health has special value insofar as it allows people to live normal human lives, reach their innate potential, and participate meaningfully in society.[4]

Legal analysis has typically framed the value of life in terms of mistakes in punishment: How certain must we be that someone is guilty before we condemn them to death?[5] "Better that ten guilty persons escape than that one innocent suffer,"[6] wrote the famous English jurist William Blackstone. (The Bible makes similar calculations. After God tells Abraham of his intention to destroy Sodom, Abraham convinces God that the city should be saved if there are at least ten righteous men living there. Alas, there were not.) Benjamin Franklin proposed sparing 100 guilty men to save one innocent man, and some jurists have proposed values as high as 1,000. This valuation is done by introspection more than calculation.

Economists have also attempted to place a value on life. The traditional economic analysis values health as the amount that a person will earn over their lifetime. Sir William Petty in 1690 was the first economist to take this approach.[7] Petty calculated the value of life as the amount of income a person would generate over 20 years of work ("The Mass of Mankind being worth Twenty Years purchase"). The implied value of a person in 1690 was about $150 in today's dollars. Many courts use a similar calculation. In litigation, the value of lost life or health impairment is often taken to be the amount a person would have earned over their remaining life span.

This methodology is not very appealing. It implies that there is no value to keeping older people alive, for example, because they are not working. Similarly, it implies that health to the rich is worth more than health to the poor, because the rich will produce goods of greater dollar value. Both of these implications violate our basic sense of fairness. The values underlying the religious and ethical views, reflecting the preciousness of human beings, are closer to what we want. People value longer, higher-quality life because health itself is a valuable goal. But how can we turn these values into practical equations?

The place to start is to quantify the health associated with different medical conditions. We all have a good sense of what it means to be healthy or sick, but we rarely make this explicit. Being more precise is the first step in valuing health. Consider the following hypothetical person:

> Tom is a 62-year-old white male with a high school education. Last year, he suffered a heart attack. Even after receiving medical care, he has a number of physical impairments. He has difficulty walking more than a quarter mile, is out of breath after climbing a flight of stairs, and cannot play for a long time with his grandchildren. Tom's doctor tells him he will probably live another ten years, and the condition will not improve in that time. His mental functioning is fine, however, and he is able to socialize with friends and relatives. His health does not limit his weekly poker game with friends.

We all agree that Tom is in less than perfect health. But how much worse?

One way to quantify Tom's health is by considering a trade-off: Suppose you are in Tom's position. Rather than living your remaining years with these limitations, however, you can choose to give up some of those years to live without the disability. How many of the ten years would you be willing to give up to be in better health?

This question is called a time trade-off. It is a way of converting quality of life into years of good health. There is no right answer to the time trade-off. Some people are unwilling to give up even a day of life for improved quality; others value quality a great deal. Everyone has a different scale. To determine a value for the population as a whole, it helps to think about how the average person would respond.[8] Because heart attacks affect a wide cross section of the population, the average person's views on them can represent those of society as a whole.

Suppose that the typical person would be willing to live eight years in good health instead of ten years in Tom's condition. We can say that Tom has eight years of "quality-adjusted life" that he can expect to live. The concept of quality-adjusted life years (QALYs) is commonly used in the medical field as a way to quantify the effect of different health states.[9] An entire branch of medicine has sprung up to measure the QALYs of different conditions.

The QALY measure can be used to determine the effect of medical interventions on health. Suppose that Tom is a candidate for a new heart attack surgery that costs $10,000. If he receives the surgery, he will be able to engage in more physical activities and play with his grandchildren. Suppose that Tom's life after surgery would be the equivalent of nine quality-adjusted years instead of eight. The surgery would thus generate one additional year of quality-adjusted life, at a cost of $10,000.

We can then compare the benefits of the new heart attack surgery with other medical interventions. If the alternative to treating heart attacks is providing more psychotherapy for depressed younger people, we would figure out how many quality-adjusted life years the depression care would bring. If $10,000 spent treating depressed teens would improve quality-adjusted life by four years, one could argue that the money would be better spent on that. If the benefits were only half a year, the heart attack care would be more valuable.

If the only choice we faced was how to allocate the resources we have now, we could stop at this point. The quality-of-life improvement of different interventions tells us which treatments are most valuable. But we often have to make other trade-offs. Is one year of quality-adjusted life to older people worth more or less than a year to teenagers? There are also trade-offs outside the medical sector. Is it better to spend the $10,000 on heart attacks or on building additional public parks? To answer this question, we need to be able to express the quality-of-life improvement in monetary terms.

Measuring health states is difficult; valuing them is even harder. How can we possibly value additional years of survival? Fortunately, the situation is not as hopeless as it first seems. When contemplating the value of life, we think first of the extremes. What would we give up to save a friend in desperate need? Most people would give as much as they could afford. The insurance setting we are considering makes things easier, however. The question in this case becomes instead: Are we willing to pay more throughout our lives so that if we have a heart attack we can receive a new therapy? The need is not immediate and the cost will not bankrupt us, so we can consider the situation more rationally.

If the cost of guaranteeing access to the heart attack care were $5 per year, almost everyone would want it. Fewer would sign up if the cost were $5,000 per year, not because people could not afford it— most could—but because other goods are valued too. The value for the typical person is probably between these two figures.

Rather than considering hypotheticals, economists prefer to look at the choices that people make. What do the insurance policies that people actually choose imply about how people value better health? The difficulty of unraveling exactly what is in insurance policies makes using this information difficult to interpret however. Fortunately, there are more clear-cut examples. Consider peoples' willingness to pay for an air bag in a car. Air bags are now standard on new cars, but they did not use to be. When air bags were optional, people had the choice of buying one at a cost of about $300, or not. Many people wanted an air bag at that price; enough did so that we did not protest when the government made them mandatory. It turns out that air bags save the life of one driver in 10,000.[10] Paying $300 to save one person in 10,000 is equivalent to paying $3 million for each life saved. Thus, the air bag suggests that most people value a life at at least $3 million.[11]

There are various examples like that of the air bag: whether one buys a fire alarm for a house, the choice between working in a riskier or safer job, and so on. A number of economic studies have inferred the value of additional life from these examples. The $3 million estimated above is relatively typical. Across a range of studies, a common conclusion is that the implied value of remaining life ranges from $3 million on the low side to $7 million on the high side, with an average of perhaps $5 million.[12] Most health economists use a number like this.

For our purposes, we care about years of life more than life as a whole, because medical interventions are frequently evaluated that way. The new heart attack treatment extends Tom's life by one year. The value of a year is what is needed. We can translate values of remaining life into a year of life by dividing by the number of years remaining. For example, a person who values their remaining life at $4 million and has a remaining life expectancy of 40 years implicitly values each year at $100,000. Such a value is typical. Most studies value a year of life at $75,000 to $150,000. I use $100,000 as the value of a year in good health, which is approximately in the middle.

There is another way, presented by economist William Nordhaus, to reach this conclusion.[13] Suppose you are offered a choice between all the consumption gains that occurred between 1950 and today—better cars, computers, televisions, and so on—or all the health improvements that have been made—nine years of life and better health while alive. Which would you choose? Informal surveys suggest that people find this choice difficult to make. The two are of roughly equal value. Adjusted for inflation, annual income has increased by about $25,000 per person since 1950, or perhaps $750,000 over a person's lifetime. If that value is equivalent to nine years of life, the implied value for each year is just under $100,000.

The $100,000 estimate is not the same for everyone. Some people value health more than others, just as some find particular conditions more disabling than others. For policy purposes, however, the average valuation is what we care about most. It captures the views of the typical person.[14] Clearly, this value of a year of life is an estimate, not an exact figure. It is a bit like asking someone what the weather is like outside—they can give a reasonable idea, but not an exact temperature. In working with the value of health, I pay particular attention to uncertainty about the true value. It would be a mistake to draw sharp conclusions based on an estimate.

One hundred thousand dollars is a lot of money. It is more than the typical person will earn in a year. This is especially noticeable since the benefit is not cash income that will show up in someone's bank account. Rather, it is the pleasure people get by living longer, healthier lives. How can a year of life be worth more than a person will earn in that year?

While this seems contradictory, in fact it is not. One point to note is that in these settings, people are spreading health care payments over their entire life. Someone who is willing to pay $2,000 each year so that they can have access to the new heart attack care is likely to pay $100,000 over the course of their lifetime ($2,000 for 50 years). Because it is spread out, the burden is smaller in any year. More fundamentally, people are willing to give up more than their annual income to be in better health. The only constraint is that they can't give up more than they could ever earn.

Consider the analogy with vacations. Most people spend more on a week's vacation than they could afford to spend if they were on vacation permanently—even if they still earned their regular salary. People are willing to cut back on their consumption at home to enjoy vacation more. The problem occurs if vacations get so extended that there is little money available for anything else. At that point, people have to be more frugal on vacations.

The same is true of health. We are willing to pay a lot for some improvements in health. That is fine, provided our income is high enough to pay for other goods as well. We would have a problem however, if we spent too much on health, and thus had little for everything else. At some point, the trade-off would no longer be worth it, and the value of health improvements would be low.

We are not at that point now. The value of health that people express in their choices about air bags, fire alarms, and the like show that health is still valued very highly relative to other things we can buy. In the future, we might run up against this constraint, although I suspect we will not.

The value of life we have calculated to this point is the value to the person affected and to his or her family. This is implicit in the choice about whether to buy an air bag or take other safety precautions.

There is another component to health improvements, however: the impact of health changes for one person on the financial status of everyone else.

Let's return to Tom. Suppose that Tom wanted to continue working, but his heart condition kept him from doing so. As a disabled nonworker, Tom would receive disability support of perhaps $20,000 per year. Further, he would not be earning income and thus not be paying taxes. All told, the cost to society of Tom's being ill is about $30,000 a year. If the new therapy allows Tom to return to work, the rest of us would be $30,000 richer. This $30,000 is an additional benefit of the heart attack care, beyond the value of better health to Tom.

Economists term this effect an externality: When one person does something that influences the economic circumstances of others, the costs and benefits of that action for other people need to be taken into account. Externalities may be positive or negative. Allowing Tom to leave disability and return to work is a positive externality. Extending life among nonworkers, as would occur by enabling Tom to live to increasingly older ages, is a negative externality, since retired people collect public transfers (Social Security, Medicare, and sometimes Medicaid), but do not pay as much in taxes as they collect.

The average elderly person receives about $10,000 in transfer income annually. Thus, the net value of a year of quality-adjusted life to the elderly is roughly $90,000—$100,000 of improved health to the individual less the $10,000 of additional support costs. Fortunately, this value is still positive; society is better off having older people alive than not. I include both the direct benefits and the financial effects on others when I evaluate medical advances. The direct benefits are generally far larger, however.

Many of the costs and benefits of medical interventions come in the future. Treating someone who is sick today may extend their life, but it does so several years down the road. Like all values in the future, the costs and benefits of medical innovation need to be discounted to the present. Economists use a range of discount rates to make this adjustment. Three percent, roughly the inflation-adjusted yield on fairly safe investments such as U.S. Treasury bonds, is a common value. I discount the costs and benefits of future medical interventions at this rate.

The methodology for evaluating medical care is complex in detail but simple in concept. Medical advance has a cost and a benefit. The cost is the money spent, which cannot be used for other goods that we want. The benefits are the value of a longer and higher-quality life to the person receiving the care, plus the effects of those health changes on others. Conceptually, that is all there is to it.

The framework I have presented is used by many health care experts, but not all.[15] It is worth laying out the objections to make clear what is happening. One objection is the difficulty of actually performing the calculations. Determining QALY weights requires that individuals value health states that they may know little about. How many people can really imagine what their life would be like if they were paralyzed? Those without use of their limbs, on the other hand, may be sufficiently adapted to the condition that they are unable to appreciate what a newly paralyzed person would experience. There is also uncertainty in how to value a life. How many people really know the effect of air bags on mortality or the risks of their job? While this critique is important, any method for valuing health requires assumptions. The key is to make certain that the results are not too dependent on any one particular set of results.

Even if we can solicit preferences accurately, peoples' preferences may not be the same at all times. For example, teenagers might not care about years lived beyond age 70, but those same teens will start to care about late-life health as they near middle age. Which set of preferences should count—the teenager's or the adult's? There is no theoretically correct answer to this. Some people believe that individual autonomy reigns supreme and we should take preferences as they are. Others argue for using the adult's preferences, as a more mature person. Implicitly, the approach outlined here uses the adult's preferences. Most of the studies of the value of health are based on adults. Thus, their preferences are weighted more than those of children and teens. I find this to be the right decision, but some do not agree.

Most fundamentally, some people object to the very idea of valuing health based on what individuals perceive, rather than on a broader social conception of what health means in society. Health is a special good, and it may reflect values beyond individual perception. Good health may be essential to functioning in a democracy, to living a decent life, or to reaching one's innate potential. Individual valuations do not necessarily consider this. To take just one example, we may feel that the elderly have earned the most advanced medical care possible, even if quality-of-life considerations do not suggest providing a lot of care to them.

Health does have a special role in society, and we all feel the tug for this broader valuation. One of the questions to consider as we see the results is how the quality-of-life answers compare to our innate sense of medical care priorities. Of course, there are multiple innate views. But I believe that the results seem to be reasonable guides to our social conception, for reasons that will be made clearer in the analysis.

We can use this methodology to evaluate the hypothetical heart attack treatment we have been considering for Tom. The cost of the therapy is $10,000 per person. The benefit is one year of quality-adjusted life. Valued at $90,000 per year (assuming that Tom would be retired anyway and collecting $10,000 in Social Security and Medicare), the treatment yields a value of $90,000. Accounting for the fact that some of the health benefits are not realized until the future lowers this value in today's terms, but not by a great deal. The net is about $80,000 of benefits. This is substantially greater than the cost. Thus, the technological advance is worth the money.

Tom's case was presented as a hypothetical, but in fact it is not. The story behind it is integral to my views about the medical system. I noted earlier the year I spent working on the Clinton administration's health plan. When I returned to academic life, I wanted to research the value of the medical system. When we spend more on medical care, are we getting enough to justify it? To address these questions, I decided to focus on one particular condition, so that I could really learn what medical spending was buying. After discussions with colleagues, I decided that heart attack care was a good starting point. Spending on heart attacks has increased rapidly over time, as treatments have become more sophisticated. Further, there are good data on health outcomes. I formed a research group with three other people to consider the heart attack case: Mark McClellan of the Food and Drug Administration, Joseph Newhouse of Harvard, and Dahlia Remler of Columbia.

The four of us gathered data from the mid-1980s through the late 1990s, the lengthiest period for which statistics were available.[16] The average heart attack cost about $12,000 to treat in the mid-1980s; costs increased by about $10,000 through the late 1990s. Along with the costs, though, came clear benefits. In that decade and a half, life expectancy after a heart attack rose by about one year. We suspected that quality of life for heart attack survivors was improving as well, but we did not have good data on quality, so we considered only the length of life.

The trade-off was thus $10,000 of increased spending for one additional year of life. At the time, we assumed a very low value for a year of life—$25,000, rather than the $100,000 noted previously. The value was low to reflect the fact that the quality of that additional year was not always so high. Even with such a low value, however, the benefits of medical advances were more than twice the costs. With a higher value of life—the $90,000 used here, for example— the ratio would be even greater. The conclusion is clear: We spend a lot more on heart attack care than we used to, but we get even more in return.

We were startled by the starkness of these conclusions and quickly published our results.[17] To our great pleasure, other people found our results as enlightening as we did. From my biased vantage point, I believe it has caused people to back off from the reflexive view that more medical spending is necessarily bad.

The clarity of these results spurred me on. If heart attack care was worth it, what about other areas of medicine in which spending has increased just as rapidly? Has that spending been worth it too? In the time since the heart attack study, I have looked at a wide range of medical technologies, examining the costs and benefits associated with them. The next few chapters summarize my findings. The conclusions generally bear out the heart attack study: We spend a lot on medicine, but we get more in return. That is not to say that everything is good. There is a good deal of waste. But a central feature of the medical system is the increasing value it provides over time.

3

SUCCESS AND FAILURE AT
THE BEGINNING OF LIFE

Baby Noelle was born at the edge of viability.[1] She emerged at 25 weeks, weighing a mere 1 lb., 13 oz. Very few babies born at this weight survive; many of Noelle's contemporaries did not.

Noelle's mother was in her early forties when Noelle was born (in 2000). She had had three previous miscarriages, and so was watched carefully. After an uneventful pregnancy, Noelle's mother went into labor in the twenty-fourth week. She was immediately admitted to a good Boston hospital, restricted to bed, and given drugs to delay birth and speed up the infant's development. Several days later, Noelle was born by emergency cesarean section.

Noelle's most immediate problem was breathing. Her lungs, on the verge of collapse, were incapable of transporting enough oxygen into the blood stream. Respiratory distress syndrome, as it is called, is a leading cause of infant death. Noelle was treated with bovine surfactant, a chemical taken from cows that keeps the lungs open. She made it through her first day.

Too young to eat on her own, Noelle was fed intravenously at first and later through a feeding tube. Throughout her first few weeks of life, she received phototherapy to prevent jaundice and had ultrasounds to check for bleeding in the brain. Despite her small size, Noelle progressed well. Nineteen days after birth, however, she suffered a setback, developing necrotizing entercolitis, an inflammation of the lining of the bowel that can prevent the absorption of nourishment and the elimination of waste. Untreated, entercolitis can lead to infection and death. Fortunately, the problem was spotted in time. Doctors operated and gave her antibiotics. By 36 days old, Noelle had improved sufficiently to resume tube feeding.

After more improvement in the hospital, she was at last allowed to go home, to the great pleasure and relief of her parents and doctors. Several months later, she continued to do well. Noelle is one of a growing number of medical miracles.

Noelle's first few months were miraculous, and also very expensive. The total cost was $192,634. This is above average for babies of her size (a typical cost is about $100,000; Noelle was more expensive because of the various surgeries), but not unusually so.

Is it worth it to spend so much on babies like Noelle? Could we have done better? If not spent on Noelle, the money could have bought health insurance for 40 poor families, or textbooks for several hundred children. These are very valuable as well.

Progress in infant survival has been profound. In 1900, one in every ten babies died in the first year of life. Today, fewer than one in a hundred do. Knowing a family in which an infant died was once commonplace; now it is rare.[2] The conquest of infectious disease was the major factor in infant mortality declines in the first half of the twentieth century. A combination of public health advances such as improved sanitation and clean water, increased nutrition, and antibiotics led to dramatically fewer infant deaths.

By 1950 infectious disease mortality was low for infants. Infant mortality remained high, however, because of the substantial number of low-birth-weight infants. Low birth weight is generally defined as less than 2,500 grams, or around five and a half pounds. Most such babies are born prematurely and are at risk for a variety of complications, most importantly respiratory distress. Premature infants typically have difficulty breathing, which can often be fatal.

In 1950 there was little that medicine could do for premature infants. There were some incubators (an offshoot of the technology used for baby chickens), and primitive attempts to provide enough oxygen and warmth. But the overall state of science was poor. Noted physician Clement Smith remarked in 1955, "Most of us who work in neonatal pediatrics are distressingly familiar with the sight of a small infant surrounded by a fog of vapor within a closed tent or incubator. The situation perhaps symbolizes the present state of my subject which is essentially a very small body of facts enveloped in a misty atmosphere of speculation which is walled off from its surroundings by a rigid container of prejudices."[3]

Infants like Noelle rarely survived. In 1963, for example, First Lady Jackie Kennedy gave birth to a baby boy, born at 32 weeks and weighing four and a half pounds (four times larger than Noelle). He too had respiratory distress syndrome, for which there were few treatments. Patrick Bouvier Kennedy died a day and a half later.

Since then, medicine has progressed to include the vast array of technologies available today. Incubator design has improved continuously and is now situated in neonatal intensive care units. Ventilators providing oxygen at the right pressure and phototherapy preventing jaundice both date from the 1970s. Corticosteroids to speed up infant development and tocolytics to delay labor were developed in the 1980s. The late 1980s and 1990s saw the widespread use of surfactant to prevent respiratory distress syndrome, and drugs to substitute for surgery for certain heart abnormalities.

The armamentarium of medicine is much greater than it used to be, but also more expensive. I have evaluated the costs and benefits of care for low-birth-weight infants along with Ellen Meara, a professor at Harvard Medical School.[4] In 1950 there were few costs for low-birth-weight infants: When little can be done, little is spent. Today, the costs are much higher. Noelle is not typical, but she is not out of the ballpark either—families can rack up bills of hundreds of thousands of dollars. Fortunately, bills of this magnitude usually occur in only the very smallest of babies. For low-birth-weight infants as a whole, medical costs in the neonatal period average about $30,000.

In addition, there are long-term medical costs of caring for low-birth-weight infants who suffer complications.[5] Up to a third of infants born at the edge of viability will suffer severe impairments, ranging from cerebral palsy to blindness to mental retardation.[6] A high-end estimate is that the additional lifetime costs of medical care needed for low-birth-weight infants is about $40,000 (roughly $1,000 per year). In total, therefore, we spend perhaps $70,000 more on medical expenses per low-birth-weight infant than we did in 1950.

Are the benefits enough to justify these costs? Low-birth-weight infants live significantly longer than they used to. Mortality for low-birth-weight infants has fallen by three-quarters since 1950, from 18 per hundred to 5 per hundred. Although only 7 percent of infants are born at a low birth weight, survival improvements for low-birth-weight infants account for two-thirds of overall infant survival.

We can measure the medical contribution to the change in low-birth-weight survival by looking at survival within birth-weight categories. Factors such as whether the mother smoked or drank during pregnancy, the environment in which the family lives, and the nature of previous pregnancies influence the gestational age and birth weight of infants, but once the baby is born, medical care is almost the only factor that is known to influence survival. Medical technology's effect on survival is particularly important in the first month of life, a period of time termed neonatal mortality. It is this component of mortality that I examine.

There has been remarkable improvement in birth-weight-specific neonatal survival since 1950 (see table).[7] Mortality rates for the smallest infants, those under 1,000 grams, or roughly two pounds, fell from 90 percent in 1950 to about 40 percent today. Mortality for the next largest infants (1,000 to 1,500 grams), about two to three pounds, fell from 55 percent to 5 percent.

To place a value on this medical advance, beyond the hours of happiness it has brought to parents and families, we need to translate it into additional years of life lived. Even today, babies born with low birth weight tend to live fewer years than normal-birth-weight babies, about 20 percent fewer, according to recent estimates.[8] Still, a typical low-birth-weight survivor can expect to live about 70 years on average. Since 1950, the average low-birth-weight infant lives about 15 years longer now because of medical advances than he or she did previously.

But what about the quality of those years? Physicians and ethicists have raised concerns about the quality of life of low-birth-weight infants, and with good reason. At the margin of viability, about

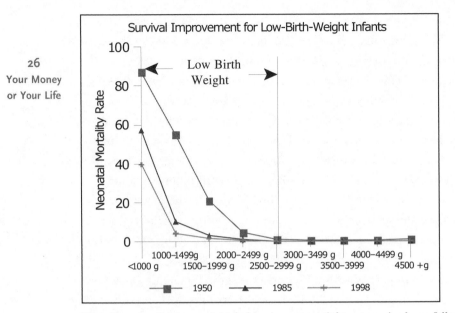

Mortality rates for low weight babies in most weight categories have fallen by over 50 percent. (United States Department of Health and Human Services, Centers for Disease Control and Prevention, National Center for Health Statistics)

one-third of infants have severe developmental problems, including cerebral palsy, mental retardation, and blindness. Another third have minor problems, such as minor learning impairments or slow development. Even with such problems, however, quality of life can still be high. One study showed that nearly three-quarters of low-birth-weight adolescents (or their parents) rated the adolescents' health as excellent or nearly so, just below the share for normal-birth-weight adolescents.[9] Increased survival of very low-birth-weight infants results in a greater share of infants with complications. On the other hand, infants at the higher end of the low-birth-weight range face very high rates of complications, but medical advances have reduced these complications.

These two effects roughly offset each other. Quality of life for the average low-birth-weight survivor is about the same as it was in 1950. Including quality and length of life, quality-adjusted life expectancy for the average low-birth-weight infant increased about 13 years between 1950 and today, only two years less than the increase in the number of years lived.

In total, therefore, $70,000 of increased spending bought 13 years of quality-adjusted life. Is this a good deal? I estimated in the previous chapter that the value of additional life years is about $100,000 per year. From this we need to subtract the additional nonmedical costs of caring for low-birth-weight infants, including special education, and sometimes disability. For the severely impaired, therefore, the benefits of life extension are only $75,000. Adding up the additional years with this value yields a benefit of $350,000 per low-birth-weight infant.[10]

The $350,000 in benefits is substantially greater than the $70,000 in additional costs. In investment terms, every dollar invested has yielded $5 in better health. Technology for low-birth-weight infants is costly, but it is clearly worth the cost.

What is most impressive about this number is how large it is. A private company would be happy with a benefit of $1.20 per dollar spent. Governments are usually happy with a return of $1.10. The return here is an order of larger magnitude. These returns are so large that the uncertainties inherent in the calculation do not seem very important. For example, a year of life could be worth only half what the literature suggests and the spending would still be overwhelmingly worth it.

Finding that medical advance is worth the cost does not imply that relying on medical technology was the best approach we could have taken. Treating low-birth-weight infants when they are born is an expensive way to extend life. Are there cheaper ways to accomplish the same goal? The answer is yes, which we can see by focusing on the sources of low birth weight.

The most important risk factor for low birth weight is maternal smoking. Women who smoke while pregnant are twice as likely to have a low-birth-weight baby as those who do not. Rather than focusing on saving lives through neonatal care, suppose we instead invested more in smoking cessation programs—providing self-help materials to help women quit, following-up regularly to address problems, and paying for cessation aids? A number of programs like this has been tried experimentally.[11] The cost of these programs is modest, about $50 per woman. The benefits are large; significant numbers of women stop smoking in the programs. In the typical program, enough women stop smoking that the smoking intervention programs are more cost-effective than neonatal intensive care. Per life saved, smoking cessation programs cost only one-third as much as neonatal intensive care.

Added to these lower costs are potential savings in the costs of neonatal care. Avoiding low-birth-weight births results in lower use of neonatal intensive care. Some researchers argue that the savings are sufficiently large that smoking cessation programs could actually save money, even as they improve health.[12]

And yet, such programs are used only sparingly. Most doctors counsel pregnant women to quit smoking, but the advice is rarely followed up systematically. Few health plans pay for smoking cessation programs or help women enroll in them. There is little nurse or physician follow-up to make sure women quit. For many people, quitting an addictive habit requires more than just exhortation. But exhortation is all that most women get.

A medical intervention that was shown in clinical trials to save lives and improve quality of life would be adopted right away. A social program that does the same is not. We shall encounter this problem time and again in looking at the medical system. High-tech medical intervention is routine; less intensive programs struggle to be accepted.

————————

Smoking cessation is not the only intervention that could reduce costs. Regular prenatal care could as well, by spotting problems early on and intervening to correct them. A 1985 report by the Institute of Medicine argued this case.[13] The Institute of Medicine estimated that every dollar spent on prenatal care could save $3.38 in caring for high-need babies. Prenatal care, according to the report, was the ultimate free lunch.

The Institute of Medicine report was a bombshell. A distinguished group of scientists had concluded that we could improve health and save money at the same time. The report led to a major change in public policy. In the decade following the report, the Medicaid program was expanded to allow more women in working-poor families to qualify for Medicaid to take advantage of these possible savings. Nearly half of all women giving birth in the United States today are eligible for Medicaid coverage when they are pregnant. Very few women giving birth are without insurance.

Nearly two decades later, we can evaluate the impact of this program. Did it improve outcomes? Were costs saved? The bottom line is that infant health improved somewhat, but money was not saved.[14] The "free" lunch turned out to come with a multibillion dollar price tag.

The reasons that the program failed to live up to expectations are revealing. One reason is that the program wasn't able to enroll only women who were previously uninsured. Among the working-poor population, a substantial share of women already had private insurance coverage. Some of these women responded to the Medicaid expansion by switching from private coverage to Medicaid, or becoming uninsured with the knowledge that Medicaid was available when needed.[15] When women substitute public insurance for private insurance, Medicaid spending rises, but there are no health benefits.

More importantly, the program didn't work as intended because use of prenatal care did not increase as envisioned. Nearly a third of the women who obtained coverage as a result of the Medicaid expansions enrolled in the last month of pregnancy—many after admission to the hospital to give birth.[16] Many women who received care earlier did not get care regularly enough. Care received this late or sporadically has few health benefits.

The government is partly to blame for this failure, as it did not alert enough women to the opportunities of the program. But government is not the sole problem; the medical system deserves blame as well. The medical system is so difficult to use that even determined women have trouble accessing it. A task as simple as scheduling an appointment and arranging baby-sitting can be prohibitive for many poor women; their lives are too chaotic to meet the rigidities of the medical world. The behavioral changes they need to make—dietary changes, reduced smoking and alcohol intake—are also difficult, and they receive no help with those changes. The premise of the Medicaid expansions was that giving women health insurance was enough. That is not the case.

A better health care system would recognize the need for outreach and provide it. Scheduling and follow-up would be easy. Coordination across providers, to deal with complications as they arise, would be seamless. Behavioral changes such as smoking cessation and diet modification would be promoted through physician and nurse outreach. Reconfiguring the system in this way would make it vastly more effective. The system doesn't do this, and we pay the price.

When asked why they do not provide these services, physicians have a uniform answer: They are not paid to provide them, and so cannot afford to invest in them. Physicians counsel patients in their office and encourage appropriate behavioral change. Harassed by insurers and pressed for time, however, that is all that the typical doctor can afford; they cannot do for patients what they know needs to be done. This just pushes the puzzle back a step, though. Insurers could pay doctors for these services, reimbursing them for outreach and rewarding successful follow-up. Why don't they? Again, the answer is money. Insurers are paid to cut spending, not improve health. Thus, they focus on managing the services provided, not encouraging more care. The financial incentives are perverse, creating a medical system that does not work as well as it might.

Private insurance and Medicaid are equivalent on this score. Each pays for medical care for pregnant women, but neither does so in the right way. Both government and the private sector will have to change to make the system work better.

Of course, even partly effective programs can still be worth the expense. That appears to be the case here. More babies survived the neonatal period as a result of the Medicaid expansions—not an enormous number, but some. Because life is valued so highly, the benefits of saving additional babies justify the added cost.[17] We didn't save money, but it was still the right thing to do. Government, to its credit, has virtually eliminated the problem of lack of insurance among women giving birth.

Still, considering infant mortality shows the strengths and weak-nesses of the medical system. On the one hand, we have invested a lot in a set of intensive technologies that have brought significant benefits. On the other hand, we could do better by investing in lower-tech care and a system that works better. Saving Noelle was good, but preventing more low-birth-weight cases would be even better.

4

THE POWER OF THE PILL: PROZAC AND THE REVOLUTION IN MENTAL HEALTH CARE

Harvard University, where I teach, experienced a horrible tragedy in late May 1995. Final exams had just ended, and commencement was barely a week away. Warm weather and sunshine enveloped the campus, and most students happily looked forward to their summer breaks. But one student did not. Sinedu Tadesse, a junior from Ethiopia, was upset that her roommate, Trang Ho, had decided not to room with her the following year.

Sinedu was not particularly happy, with few close friends and little family in the area. She also suffered from mental illness. Melanie Thernstrom, a former Harvard student and writer who wrote about the case,[1] suggested that Sinedu suffered from depression and schizotypal personality disorder, the latter characterized by an inability to form close relationships and the occurrence of paranoid thoughts and, occasionally, psychotic episodes. People with this personality disorder can become psychotic in response to stress, especially if they are also depressed.

That is apparently what happened to Sinedu. On the morning of May 28, the day that she and Trang were to move out of their dorm room, she stabbed her roommate 45 times, killing her, and then proceeded to hang herself. Two students, seemingly destined for wonderful lives, were dead.

The horror of the situation stunned the Harvard community. There was a great deal of soul-searching about what went wrong and how it could have been prevented. While the magnitude of the loss was great, however, no one was surprised by the presence of mental illness at Harvard. Mental illness is among the most common health problems of teenagers and young adults. Murder of one student by another is rare, but suicide is not—major universities like Harvard average about one per year. The mental health service at Harvard, serving a population of about 30,000, has over 20,000 visits each year. As most professors will attest, when there is a poorly performing student in class—one who fails exams and problem sets, attends class infrequently, and appears out of touch—there is often a mental health issue involved.

Doing poorly in one class is not so problematic. Dropping out of college or never attending in the first place, losing time at work, attempting suicide, or having a family breakup, are more serious consequences. All are common for people with mental illness.

Mental illness is also extraordinarily common among the general population.[2] About one in five adults nationally, roughly 40 million people, suffers from some form of mental illness. Mental illness is second only to hypertension in prevalence in the United States. Suicide is the third leading cause of death for people aged 15 to 24, and the fifth leading cause for people aged 25 to 44. We spend about $70 billion annually on mental health.

The good news is that mental illness is much more treatable now than it was even 20 years ago. Medications and therapies developed in the past half century, and particularly in the past two decades, have moved it from a shameful problem hidden in the closet to a routine chronic condition with ready treatments. The bad news is that we overuse some mental health care, and we dramatically underuse other care. The state of care for mental illness is thus a good indicator of the value and the problems in the medical system.

Unlike physical ailments, mental health often cannot be readily observed. For this reason, mental illness has been stigmatized as being less of an illness than physical ailments.[3] Historically, mental illness was ascribed to bad character or God's will; it was not until the twentieth century that science embraced mental illness as a disease. And even since then, the definition of mental illness has changed as physicians have refined their understanding of what is involved in normal mental functioning. Today, mental illness encompasses a number of sub-conditions, including mood disorders such as depression and mania, cognitive disorders (Alzheimer's disease and dementia), anxiety, psychosis, and eating disorders.[4]

To get at the value of mental health treatment over time, I will focus on a single illness: major depression, or what we commonly think of as depression.[5] Mental health professionals diagnose depression using a specific set of criteria (see table). To be diagnosed as clinically depressed, the depressed state must occur daily for a minimum of two weeks. In addition, there must be at least four of eight other symptoms, including anxiety, weight change, and insomnia or hypersomnia.

The surgeon general estimates that roughly ten million adults suffer from major depression, although some estimates suggest millions more.[6] A depressive episode may strike suddenly, may occur in response to a traumatic event such as a death in the family or a work conflict, or may build up over a number of years of mild depression. Episodes of depression typically last between several weeks and several months. Untreated, 50 percent of people suffering from a first episode will have a recurrence, with subsequent episodes being even more common. The typical person with depression will have five to seven episodes over his or her lifetime, although cases of up to 40 episodes have been noted.

In 1990 about $12 billion was spent on medical treatment for depression.[7] This seems high, but it represents only 2 percent of total medical spending. The cost of depression is more than just the treatment cost, however. Since depression often strikes in the teens and mid-twenties, the disease limits educational attainment and reduces peoples' ability to work. Estimates of these "indirect costs" of illness are several times the direct costs.[8]

Standards for depression diagnosis are set by the American Psychiatric Association. To be diagnosed as depressed, a person must have five or more of the following symptoms nearly every day during the same two-week period, and this must represent a change from previous functioning. At least one of the symptoms must be either depressed mood or loss of interest or pleasure.

1. Depressed mood most of the day
2. Diminished interest or pleasure in all, or almost all, activities
3. Significant unintentional weight loss or weight gain, or a change in appetite
4. Insomnia or hypersomnia
5. Psychomotor agitation or retardation (changes in movement resulting from psychological factors)
6. Fatigue or loss of energy
7. Feelings of worthlessness or excessive or inappropriate guilt
8. Diminished ability to think or concentrate, or indecisiveness
9. Recurrent thoughts of death or suicide.

In addition, the symptoms must not be due to the direct physiological effects of a substance or general medical condition, or bereavement.

It is not entirely clear what causes depression.[9] Genetic factors are certainly important. For reasons that are not completely understood, depression is twice as common in women as in men. Theories about the underlying causes of depression fall into two groups: psychological and biological. Psychological theories date back to Sigmund Freud early in the twentieth century and view depression as a product of the psychosocial circumstances of the individual (how the person consciously or unconsciously perceives his or her environment). Freud stressed conflict with parents, but more recent theories highlight learned or perceived aspects of current relationships as well. Biological theories focus on chemical imbalances in the brain—in particular, low levels of neurotransmitters (chemicals that communicate between nerve cells). People with depression have low concentrations of neurotransmitters, particularly serotonin. The link between the psychological and biological views of depression is not clear at present, but is an active area of research.

Treatment of depression has changed immensely over time.[10] In 1950 mildly depressed people generally suffered in silence, while those with more severe mental illness were sent to mental hospitals. There, they likely received a diagnosis of schizophrenia, a catchall for severe mental illness, or perhaps something a bit more specific to depression, such as "involutional melancholia," "neurotic depression," or "neurasthenia." Diagnosis was imprecise because treatment was not particularly differentiated by diagnosis.

Treatment in mental institutions was poor, to say the least. A warehouse is a better analogy than a modern-day hospital. Consider this description from Dr. Max Fink, a psychiatrist at Hillside Hospital in New York in the 1950s:[11]

> Most schizophrenic patients were confined to hospitals, and treated with milieu- and psycho-therapies. Favorable responses were few. When the symptoms became severe, especially when the patients were psychotic, manic, suicidal, or dangers to others, electroconvulsive therapy (ECT) was given two to three times a week over six to ten weeks. . . . Patients suffered fractures, severe memory loss, and spontaneous seizures. . . . Remission rates varied from 30 percent to 80 percent of the patients treated.
>
> When ECT failed, insulin coma therapy (ICT) was considered. Insulin injections led to two to three hours of low blood sugar levels. (Insulin is a hormone that drives sugars from the blood to storage in the liver.) When blood sugar levels fall precipitously, the brain cannot sustain consciousness and the patients become stuporous. . . . Patient went gradually to sleep and then to coma. . . . Breathing became slow and stertorous. Eye movements wandered. . . . Occasional spasms of the main body muscles were seen. Sweating was severe, and temperature rose. In time, breathing became irregular, pulse rapid, and corneal and pupillary reflexes absent. Deep tendon reflexes were lost. . . . Administering glucose ended the coma . . . When a patient became conscious, his responses

would be slow, with a thick (drunken) speech. Within 15 minutes, he recognized the nurse and doctor [and] knew where he was.

[ECT and ICT] were unpleasant and dangerous. They were given without anesthesia. The ICT mortality rate varied from 1 percent to 10 percent of patients treated. Prolonged coma, in which the patient did not respond to the administration of glucose, was a constant threat.

[Lobotomy] is the surgical undercutting of the frontal lobe of the brain. It was developed in 1935 for the relief of severe agitation and obsessive-compulsive behavior. It was soon directed to patients with schizophrenia. During the 1940s and 1950s, [ECT, ICT, and lobotomy] were widely used.

Two medications changed all that. The first, discovered in France in 1950 was Chlorpromazine, which dramatically improved the functioning of patients with schizophrenia. The difference was immediate; schizophrenics taking Chlorpromazine would often begin acting normally within days of starting the medication. The second medication was Iproniazid, the first of a class of drugs known as Mono-amine Oxidase Inhibitors (MAOIs), which helped people with depression by preventing the breakdown of key chemical messengers in the brain. The antidepressive effects of Iproniazid were actually discovered by accident. The drug was used to treat tuberculosis until it was noted in the early 1950s that it elevated mood as well.[12] This finding surprised everybody, including the pharmaceutical manufacturer, which had planned to take Iproniazid off the market (a better tuberculosis drug had been developed).

The development of these medications led to major changes. For the first time, a clinical distinction was made between psychosis, disorders of perception and thought processes such as those found in schizophrenics, and mood disorders, including depression and mania. Different medications were appropriate for these two groups.[13]

Iproniazid has side effects that limit its usefulness. It can lead to hypertension crises in people eating certain foods (including aged cheese, pickled herring, and certain beans). Because of this possibility, MAOIs were once taken off the market, and are only used today when other medications have failed.

More important, therapeutically, were medications that followed Iproniazid, especially the tricyclic antidepressants, or TCAs, which work by increasing levels of the neurotransmitters norepinephrine and serotonin in the brain. The first such drug, Imipramine,[14] was approved by the Food and Drug Administration in 1959. Imipramine was initially intended to treat schizophrenia, but did not work for those patients (to the great disappointment of the pharmaceutical company that discovered it). But it did reduce depression.

TCAs have fewer side effects than MAOIs, and thus became the primary medication for treating depression. Still, TCAs have substantial side effects, including anticholinergic effects (dry mouth, constipation, blurred vision), sedation, hypotension (decreased blood pressure, dizziness upon arising), and impotence. Also, over-dosing on a TCA can be fatal, a real concern when dealing with suicidal patients. As a result of these side effects, TCAs are usually prescribed at low doses at the beginning and are increased in the first few weeks of therapy. This requires frequent trips to doctors and increased side-effects over time, each of which makes it hard for patients and physicians to manage the therapy.

The development of antidepressants led psychiatrists to rethink treatment of the less severely ill. Psychiatrists had some inkling of what this involved from World War II, when treating soldiers on the battlefield opened up the possibility of community-based care back home. After intense debate within the psychiatric community, psychiatrists ultimately accepted the importance of less severe forms of disease (this was a boon for their incomes) and began outpatient therapy. Initially synonymous with Freudian psychoanalysis, psychotherapy has flowered into a variety of techniques such as cognitive therapy, behavioral therapy, and various combinations of them. Today, there are over 250 recognized forms of psychotherapy.

Therapy of depressed patients using TCAs and psychotherapy became the mainstay of psychiatric practice from the early 1960s through the late 1980s. Use of these services was furthered by insurance programs that paid for community care, and by the deinstitutionalization movement that brought many mentally ill into the community.

Even though effective therapy was available by the 1980s, treatment of the mentally ill was still poor throughout that decade. The complexity of treatment regimens and side effects made primary care physicians leery of treating depression. Thus, the psychiatrist became the source of most mental health care, even for medication. Seeing a psychiatrist was highly stigmatized, however; many did not go, even when cost was not an issue. When medication was prescribed, doses were often too low to be clinically effective. Doses were started low to avoid side effects, but often not increased.

Diagnosis also presented various problems. The importance of depression was not uniformly accepted by primary care physicians, some of whom were biased against mental illnesses. Compounding this was the difficulty of diagnosing depression. Depressed patients often presented pain, agitation, or insomnia; physicians sometimes saw these physical manifestations but did not recognize the underlying disease.

Studies of the mental health system in the 1970s and 1980s show these failures. Only about half of patients with depression were correctly diagnosed by primary care physicians, and only a share of those correctly diagnosed were appropriately treated.[15] A major study in the early 1980s estimated that about 10 percent of patients with depression received adequate doses of antidepressant therapy for an appropriate period of time.[16] As many as 70 percent of depressed patients received no antidepressant treatment at all.[17]

The failure of the mental health system to treat people with depression adequately was clear even at the time. Clinical data on poor depression control were first reported by researchers in the 1970s.[18] Literature reviews summarizing the evidence were published in the late 1970s and 1980s.[19] There were consensus statements and calls to action. Textbooks emphasized to physicians the undertreatment of depression. But none of it worked. Through the 1980s, diagnosis of depression was not increasing. In the late 1980s, depression was still underdiagnosed and undertreated. A new plan was needed.

The change in mental health care came via a little green pill called Prozac. Prozac is a member of a relatively new class of antidepressants known as Selective Serotonin Reuptake Inhibitors, or SSRIs. As the name implies, SSRIs selectively act on serotonin levels in the brain, leaving the levels of other neurotransmitters unaffected. Serotonin seems to be the most important chemical in depression, so SSRIs are a more targeted form of therapy.

Prozac was approved by the FDA in 1987. Other drugs with similar mechanisms of action have followed, including Zoloft (1992), Paxil (1993), Luvox (1994), and Celexa (1998). A number of drugs similar to SSRIs have also been developed, including Wellbutrin (1985), Effexor (1993), and Serzone (1995).

SSRIs, TCAs, and psychotherapy have all been around long enough to be evaluated clinically, and studies show that all three work to alleviate depressive symptoms.[20] For less severe forms of depression, the three have roughly equivalent efficacy. In each case, treatment is effective in about 60 percent of cases; 35 percent of people get better taking a placebo. There is debate among researchers about whether medication or psychotherapy is better for severe cases of depression, or whether a combination of the two is better still.[21] The issue is contentious because patients' lives, not to mention the income of psychotherapists, is at stake. At this point, there is no consensus.

On the clinical side, SSRIs are no more effective than TCAs in fighting depression. Why, then, are they such a revolution in care? The answer is that SSRIs have many fewer side effects than do TCAs, making them easier for patients to sustain.[22] Further, SSRIs are started at or near their effective dose, so there is less need for dosage changes, physician visits, and frequent monitoring. Thus, SSRIs are far preferred by both patients and physicians.

Insurers are generally pleased to let patients take SSRIs rather than TCAs. SSRIs cost more per pill than do TCAs, since most SSRIs are still under patent.[23] The cost differential is about $250 per course of therapy. But the reduced need for physician visits for patients taking SSRIs makes the total cost of a course of therapy virtually the same in both cases—about $700 each per course of therapy. With equivalent cost and greater effectiveness, insurers place no barriers on SSRI use.

SSRIs also have cost advantages over psychotherapy; a full course of psychotherapy averages more than $1,000. Thus, insurers prefer medication over psychotherapy. SSRIs are more convenient for patients and involve lower out-of-pocket costs, so patients prefer medication as well. As a result of the lower patient cost and convenience, more patients complete a course of SSRI therapy than of psychotherapy. In actual practice, the average cost for using psychotherapy is about the same as for using SSRIs because most people do not complete a full course of therapy. Costs are the same, but the medication is typically more effective.

Comparing SSRIs alone with a combination of SSRIs and psychotherapy is more complex, since it is not known if the combination therapy is more effective clinically. Most insurance plans allow some combination therapy, but not unlimited amounts. Patients might be covered for some psychotherapy visits but not for ongoing care.

SSRIs are a clear therapeutic improvement. They cost the same as TCAs and psychotherapy, but have fewer side effects than TCAs and are more effective per dollar spent than psychotherapy.

SSRIs have done much more than provide a new treatment option for depressed people. They have led to a fundamental change in the public's perception of mental illness, and thus in peoples' willingness to seek treatment. While depression is still somewhat stigmatized, it bears nowhere near the stigma it once had: Depression has become a treatable disease, much like hypertension or diabetes. As a result, people are more likely to seek treatment, and physicians are more likely to diagnose depression and treat it appropriately.

The decline in stigma is hard to measure quantitatively but is readily apparent. In 1972, when Democratic vice-presidential nominee Thomas Eagleton admitted to having been hospitalized for nervous exhaustion and receiving electric shock therapy, he was forced to resign the vice-presidential nomination immediately. In the 1980s Betty Ford and Kitty Dukakis admitted to depression and substance abuse, but only after their husbands were out of the political limelight. As the 2000 presidential campaign was just beginning, however, Tipper Gore admitted to suffering from depression and receiving treatment. She was praised for saying so publicly, and there was little protest. This is not to say that we would be willing to accept a presidential candidate that had been treated for depression, but we are changing.

Survey evidence confirms this new perception. When describing a typical person with depression, three-quarters of people attribute the person's problems to a chemical imbalance in the brain and suggest that medication would help.[24] Traditional explanations for depression, such as bad character, God's will, or the way a person was raised, are no longer as common. The biological theory of depression has made its mark.

People viewing depression as a biological disease are more likely to talk to their doctor about the illness and seek treatment. Doctors who know that safe treatments are available are more likely to diagnose it. In the years since Prozac was approved, diagnosis of depression has doubled.[25]

The SSRI revolution's role in increasing treatment of people who were previously undiagnosed has greatly improved quality of life for many. The drawback of this trend is that these treatments are sometimes overused.[26] Some people taking SSRIs are only mildly depressed, for example; the literature is not clear on whether SSRIs help in such cases. Others are misdiagnosed with depression when they are not depressed. Still others take SSRIs for cosmetic reasons (a side effect of Prozac is that it sometimes results in weight loss).

To evaluate the SSRI revolution, we must compare the costs of overuse with the benefits of treating more people. On the cost side, data assembled by economists Ernst Berndt, Susan Busch, and Richard Frank[27] indicate that SSRI treatment costs about $700 per case, as noted above. The cost of depression when not diagnosed is smaller, because people receive some medical care even in the absence of a formal diagnosis. Many depressed people report back pain, insomnia, or other illnesses, for example, and are treated for those conditions. Treating those ailments might cost $100, so the net treatment cost is about $600.

The first benefit of this care is the fact that the individual is happier and in better health. Compared to no treatment, SSRI treatment reduces the time spent depressed by about ten weeks. Surveys of people with depression show very severe reductions in quality of life because of the disease. When life with and without depression is described, a typical person responds that he or she would be willing to accept about six years without depression in exchange for ten years with depression.[28] Applying a value for a year in good health of $100,000 values health improvements from less time depressed at about $6,500.

In addition to the health benefits, there are the economic benefits for society that come from depressed people being able to work and earn more.[29] Data suggest that these economic benefits amount to about $600 of additional income. The total economic benefit of increased diagnosis is thus about $7,100.

The SSRI costs will be paid for by everyone receiving treatment, but the benefits will only accrue to those for whom the therapy is effective. Since some of the people newly diagnosed with depression do not have clinical depression and thus will not benefit as much, only a share of the potential benefits will be realized. It is not known what share of people receiving antidepressants are truly depressed. Some estimates suggest that as many as 40 percent of people taking SSRIs had diagnoses for conditions other than depression.[30] Many of these patients will receive some benefit from the medication, but not as much as the intended group.

Still, even if these patients received no benefit from the antidepressant at all, the benefits of expanded treatment would be about $4,000. This substantially exceeds the $600 cost. The return is about $7 for every $1 invested. Even without complete information, it is clear that additional treatment of depression is worth the cost. Depression was so chronically underdiagnosed prior to the SSRI era that diagnosing and treating more people now is certainly valuable.

Even with the recent increase in treatment rates, diagnosis and treatment of depression remains a problem. Recent studies suggest that only about 25 percent of people with depression receive recommended levels of care.[31] That is better than the 10 percent in the pre-SSRI era, but it still leaves 75 percent without effective therapy.

Not surprisingly, the uninsured have the greatest difficulty accessing care. Uninsured people go to primary care physicians less frequently than do people with insurance, and the probability of their being diagnosed appropriately is lower. Further, mental illness is rarely a life or death matter, so emergency rooms, which are set up for acute care, are of less help. The uninsured also find it more difficult to afford medications and psychotherapy. The uninsured with mental illness are less than half as likely as the insured to receive any mental health care, and only a third as likely to receive appropriate treatment.[32] All this contributes to poorer mental health and quality of life for the uninsured.

There is a vicious cycle at work with insurance for the mentally ill. The uninsured have difficulty receiving care. When people do have mental illness, it is harder to keep insurance, since work suffers and income falls. This results in a downward spiral for many.

More drugs like Prozac will not solve the access problems of the uninsured. SSRIs cost more than what many uninsured people can afford, especially when physician visits are needed to diagnose the disease and monitor the medication. The private sector can go only so far. The government will have to do more.

Beyond the problem of lack of insurance, it is worth noting that even people with adequate insurance frequently do not get adequate care. No more than a third of depressed people with health insurance receive care up to clinical standards. Doctors miss diagnoses for that group, treatment regimens are inappropriate, and the system of accessing care is too complex. Lack of insurance is not the issue, but other factors are, including the difficulty of diagnosis, the stigma, and the hassle of using the system. The health care system will not improve the way it treats mental illness unless it makes treatment easier for the insured as well as the uninsured.

Prozac clearly revolutionized the treatment of depression. But how did it accomplish this? What is the magic in the little green pills? At heart, the Prozac example highlights the power of financial incentives in medicine.

Prescription medications cost an enormous amount to develop. The cost of a new drug can be $500 million or more. But after the drug has been developed, producing additional pills is very cheap. Pharmaceutical companies charge a lot for a pill to recoup their initial research and development, and to earn profits.

As a result of the high prices, once the drug has been developed, there are enormous incentives to get it prescribed. Every new prescription brings in a few hundred dollars of profits. Responding to this incentive, Eli Lilly (Prozac), Pfizer (Zoloft), SmithKline Beecham (Paxil), and the rest of the pharmaceutical industry spent billions of dollars getting people to see their doctors for depression and getting doctors to diagnose and treat the disease.

We have all seen the ads for antidepressant medications—formerly sad people beaming with happiness. Many people approach doctors because of the ads, and doctors are more receptive to patients with the condition as a result of pharmaceutical companies' efforts.[33] Direct-to-consumer advertisement is but the tip of the iceberg. Pharmaceutical companies spend even more "detailing" physicians—telling them about the latest medical advances and convincing them to use their medication in treating patients.

This behavior is repulsive to many analysts, and I understand why. It results in some people's believing that they need medication when they really do not. It gets others to switch from a therapy that is already working to a more expensive, newer one. It poses as a substitute doctor without knowing all the facts. Each of these are drawbacks, and they need to be addressed. But the lesson that many draw—the government should prohibit advertising and detailing and engage in its own outreach efforts—is not the right one. We need to remember the good side of this behavior—pharmaceutical company outreach gets depressed people into the doctor's office and on medication. Underdiagnosis and undertreatment were major problems with the old system. Pleading with doctors and government advisories never solved these problems. Advertising and detailing are somewhat noxious, but they do work.

There are lessons in this for medical care as a whole. Ultimately, the medical system works the way the incentives steer it. Rather than fight the system or plead for it to be otherwise, we should instead line the incentives up right so the system gives us what we want. Suppose that Medicare and private insurers paid physicians more when depressed patients were appropriately treated than when they were not, and that private insurers earned additional income from having a lower burden of depression among their enrollees. This would create financial incentives for providers to work toward effective treatment of the mentally ill. People would be encouraged to come in at appropriate times and would be given the right medications. Dropping out of therapy would be reduced. No longer would pharmaceutical companies' incentives be the only ones encouraging more use.

Treatment of the mentally ill shows the enormous effect that money can have in medicine. If we can get the financial flows right, we could do even better.

5

THE HEART
OF THE MATTER

P RESIDENT FRANKLIN D. ROOSEVELT
died of hypertension.[1] The official cause of death was a stroke; the
underlying cause was high blood pressure. Roosevelt was significantly
impaired by the disease in the last year of his life. At a time when a
world war was being fought and the postwar balance of power ne-
gotiated, Roosevelt fatigued easily, had difficulty concentrating,
became weak, lost weight, and suffered from headaches. Winston
Churchill's personal doctor remarked upon seeing Roosevelt at the
Yalta conference in 1945: "I doubt, from what I have seen, whether
he is fit for his job here."[2]

In 1945, when Roosevelt died, hypertension was essentially un-
treatable. He was given medication for his condition, but it was not
very effective. Today, there are many pharmaceuticals that would
have safely, effectively, and cheaply kept Roosevelt alive had they
been available then.

How would history be different if hypertension medication had
been available in Roosevelt's time? Some have argued that a healthy
Roosevelt could have convinced Stalin to allow peaceful elections in
Eastern Europe, saving millions of people from decades of brutal
Communist rule. Others have suggested that Roosevelt would have
shifted U.S. support from Chiang Kai-shek to Mao's China, possibly
preventing the Korean War and dramatically altering the postwar
balance of power. Even Roosevelt's cardiologist confessed, years after
Roosevelt's death, "I have often wondered what turn the subsequent

course of history might have taken if the modern methods for the control of hypertension had been available."[3]

This chapter looks at the modern methods for treating cardiovascular disease. Cardiovascular disease shows medicine at its best and its worst. On the one hand, technological advance has brought clear benefits, far above what we spend. People live longer, healthier lives because of what medical innovation has been able to do. But at the same time, there are enormous errors in the system. Some people get too much care, and others get too little. We do not achieve nearly the health gains that we might. Rectifying these errors would make the system work substantially better.

After infectious disease mortality declined in the first half of the twentieth century, cardiovascular disease, particularly diseases of the heart, became the nation's leading killer; cancer was a distant second. In mid-century, cardiovascular disease's high rate of mortality was taken as a given. Since 1950, however, cardiovascular disease mortality has declined markedly, falling by over half. This decline has contributed more than any other to the increase in life expectancy in the past few decades.

Why has this decline occurred, and what does it say about the medical system? I have explored this question with Srikanth Kadiyala, a graduate student at Harvard. We estimate that three factors are primarily responsible for lower mortality.[4] The first factor is advances in intensive medical therapies to treat acute events like heart attacks and strokes, the most severe forms of cardiovascular disease. Heart attacks, the most common cause of cardiovascular disease mortality, occur when blood flow to the heart becomes blocked by the buildup of plaque in the coronary arteries. This blockage deprives the heart of oxygen, leading to heart muscle damage and possibly death. Strokes result from impaired blood flow to the brain, either because arteries in the brain become blocked or because an artery bursts. When a blockage in the arteries occurs, the first priority is to restore blood flow to damaged areas.

In 1950 treatment of heart attacks was not very sophisticated.[5] The most famous medical textbook of the era, William Osler's *The Principles and Practice of Medicine*, started its discussion of heart attack treatment by recommending that: "Absolute rest is essential. Except in the mildest cases bed rest for at least 6 weeks should be planned from the outset."[6] It went on to recommend the patient be given morphine for pain, be warmed if in shock, and be given oxygen. That prescription was followed even in the most famous cases of the day, such as President Dwight D. Eisenhower's heart attack in 1955.[7]

We know today that bed rest is ineffective. It does not prevent further heart damage, and it can lead to other complications such as blood clots in the veins or lungs. A doctor following such a strategy now could be sued for malpractice.

Treatment of heart attacks today is much more intensive. Upon admission to a hospital, most people will be given aspirin and drugs such as heparin to thin the blood and reduce clotting, beta-blockers to reduce the workload of the heart, and thrombolytic drugs to help dissolve the clot. While aspirin is an old medication, it was not shown to be effective in treating heart attacks until the late 1980s. Heparin is also relatively old, although advances in the 1990s (low-molecular-weight heparin) have made it much more effective. Beta-blockers were developed in the 1970s. The first thrombolytics were developed in the 1970s, with newer and more effective drugs brought to the market in the 1980s.

Either immediately after a heart attack or several weeks later, patients may undergo a variety of intensive surgical procedures,[8] such as cardiac catheterization, first developed in 1959, a procedure in which dye is injected into the coronary arteries to determine the extent of arterial blockage. If the blockage detected is sufficiently severe, the patient might undergo a coronary artery bypass graft (developed in 1968), which creates a new route for blood flow around the occluded arteries, or possibly percutaneous angioplasty (developed in 1978), in which a balloon is inflated amid the clot to reopen the blocked artery. Wire mesh tubes called stents, developed in the 1990s and made famous by their use in Vice President Richard Cheney, are now typically implanted to keep the artery open. In addition to these technical changes, organizational changes such as coronary care units (developed in the 1960s) and trained emergency medical service personnel (introduced in the 1970s) have increased survival rates.

The development of these intensive treatments has had a major effect on heart attack mortality. Death in the aftermath of a heart attack has fallen by nearly three-quarters since the 1950s, largely due to increased use of intensive therapies. In total, the increased use of intensive medical therapies to treat heart attacks explains about one-third of the total reduction in cardiovascular disease mortality.

Non-acute medications, including antihypertensives (to control blood pressure), cholesterol-lowering drugs, and drugs to manage diabetes, are a second factor in improved health. These medications help prevent initial heart attacks, strokes, and recurrent attacks. Once again, the historical experience shows how important these medications have become. In 1950 there was debate about whether hypertension and high cholesterol really led to cardiovascular disease. Harrison's *Principles of Internal Medicine*, the book that would become the Bible on basic medicine, noted different schools of thought on the topic. Even people who believed that hypertension and high cholesterol led to disease did not have a cutoff in mind for safe levels of blood pressure and cholesterol. Rather, Harrison stressed that treatment should be based on the complications the patient was having. Those with chest pain or other overt signs of heart disease should have their blood pressure and cholesterol controlled; others should not. We now know that this was a poor strategy. By the time of physical manifestation, most of the damage has already been done.

Diagnosis didn't really matter much, however, because treatment was so poor. A 1948 pamphlet on treating hypertension recommended that hypertensive patients slow down and that they rest around midday.[9] Some medications were available, but they were not very practical. Treatment required three or four injections daily and had severe side effects. Other therapies included sympathectomy, severing the nerves to blood vessels (a surgery with great risk of complication!); and pyrogen therapy, inducing fever to lower blood pressure. But as the pamphlet noted, treatment was little better and potentially more dangerous than the "thousand and one advertized cures and remedies for hypertension." It was far more common for patients to receive lifestyle recommendations only—cut salt use and reduce weight. This is generally sound advice. For people with high cholesterol, treatment was largely dietary as well—reduce fat and cholesterol intake and overall weight. This is also sound, but not always successful. There were few effective treatments beyond life-style changes.

Knowledge improved over the next few decades. Particularly important for this advance was the Framingham Heart Study, begun in 1948 to look for "the" cause of cardiovascular disease. The study has followed a group of people in Framingham, Massachusetts—and now follows their offspring as well.[10] In the early 1960s, the Framingham study confirmed that hypertension did lead to cardiovascular disease. Accompanying this advance in knowledge were the first convenient and effective medications to treat hypertension. Oral diuretics, developed in the late 1950s and 1960s, did not require injections or hospitalization, and had less side effects. Subsequent years saw the discovery of beta-blockers (most were developed in the 1970s), calcium channel blockers (1980s), ACE inhibitors (1980s and 1990s), and other medications. The Framingham study and clinical trials of the new medications allowed physicians for the first time to diagnose normal and high blood pressure and to treat hypertension before it led to severe complications.[11]

Knowledge about cholesterol management followed a similar history. Little was known about cholesterol complications until the 1950s and 1960s, when research by epidemiologist Ancel Keys showed that cholesterol intake was related to cardiovascular disease: Communities with high consumption of fats and cholesterol had high rates of heart disease, while communities with lower consumption did not.[12] Keys made the cover of *Time* magazine for his studies. The Framingham Heart Study confirmed the findings.

Medication therapy progressed with disease knowledge. Nicotinic acid, which reduces the production of some types of cholesterol, was the primary treatment for high cholesterol in the 1950s and 1960s. Side effects of this therapy were severe, however, including flushing and hot flashes, nausea, gastrointestinal problems, and liver problems. In the 1970s, bile acid sequestrants and fibric acid derivatives were developed, but these too had major side effects. The revolution in cholesterol treatment came with the development of so-called statin drugs in the late 1980s. Mevacor was the first statin, approved for use in 1987; a series of other medications followed, including Lipitor, Zocor, Prevachol, and Lescol. Today, statins are among the most commonly used of all medications. They are very effective in lowering cholesterol and have few side effects.

In addition to antihypertensives and cholesterol-lowering drugs, numerous other pharmaceuticals have been developed to aid cardiovascular disease management. These drugs include aspirin to prevent heart attacks, insulin and other medications to control diabetes, oral nitrates and calcium channel blockers to improve blood flow to the heart, and antiarrhythmics to regulate the heart's rhythm. All have been added to the medical arsenal or their benefits for cardiovascular disease have become apparent, since 1950.

We can see the impact of these medications in better risk factor control and reduced disease onset. Hypertension and high cholesterol are much less common now than in 1950.[13] One-quarter fewer people develop serious cardiovascular disease than did in the 1950s. Better risk factor control and the new drugs to manage disease have also led to fewer recurrent episodes after a first heart attack or stroke. I estimate that increased use of non-acute medications explains about one-third of the total reduction in cardiovascular disease mortality since 1950.

A number of behavioral factors are also important for cardiovascular disease, including smoking, diet, alcohol consumption, and exercise. The number of people exhibiting harmful behaviors has been reduced over time, leading to improvements in health.[14]

The decline in smoking is the single most important behavioral change of the past half century. The number of smokers has fallen by a third since 1960, and people who do smoke consume fewer cigarettes.

Changes in diet have had a mixed effect on health. People have gradually begun to eat more healthfully. Fat and cholesterol consumption has fallen as a share of our diet.[15] The bacon and egg breakfast has largely been replaced by high-fiber cereal, or an oat bran muffin. Red meat is out and chicken is in. Whole milk has been replaced by lower fat or skim milk. Salt consumption has fallen,[16] along with heavy alcohol use. On the opposite side of the ledger, total caloric intake has risen markedly.[17] As a result, more Americans are obese than used to be. With the increase in obesity has come an increase in diabetes.[18]

While the effect of smoking on disease risk is clear, we do not know the effect of dietary changes on health. It is not clear, for example, whether fat consumption is really harmful for cardiovascular health,[19] or how important salt intake is for hypertension.[20] Similarly, diet may affect blood pressure differently than we thought.[21] Until these issues are resolved, we cannot calculate the precise effect of dietary change on mortality.

It is possible to guess at the importance of behavioral changes, however. On the low end, the decline in smoking explains 10 percent of reduced cardiovascular disease mortality. On the high end, acute and non-acute medical interventions such as new heart attack therapies and pharmaceuticals explain two-thirds of better health, so that lifestyle changes in total can explain, at most, one-third of the health improvements. Without additional research, which is now ongoing, we cannot be more specific than this.

Beyond medical interventions and lifestyle changes, several other factors contribute to cardiovascular disease.[22] Older people are at higher risk of disease than are younger people, for example. Because older people are a larger proportion of the population now than in 1950, however, the age effect cannot explain the reduction in cardiovascular disease mortality in the past half century. There are a number of other factors that influence disease rates, but like aging they are unlikely to explain the trend toward improved health over time.

Clear evidence supports a link between inflammation and cardiovascular disease. Physician researcher Paul Ridker has shown that people with high levels of certain inflammatory proteins are at greater risk of cardiovascular disease than those with lower levels of those proteins.[23] This suggests a possible role for infectious disease, or anti-inflammatory medications, in explaining recent trends in health. Might the decline of infectious disease a half century ago have also led to the recent improvement in cardiovascular health?

While there is not enough evidence to answer this question in detail, I suspect reduced infection rates are not likely to be a large part of the improvement in cardiovascular disease mortality. The bacteria that have been linked to cardiovascular disease are still relatively common—*Helicobacter pylori* (the cause of ulcers), *Chlamydia pneumoniae* (a bacteria also associated with respiratory disease and, potentially, Alzheimer's disease), and *Porphyromonas gingivalis* (bacteria that causes gingivitis).[24] Other bacteria have declined in prevalence, but not these.[25] The factors that have been proposed to limit the body's inflammatory response include lifestyle changes such as weight control, diet, exercise, and reduced smoking, and use of cholesterol-lowering pharmaceuticals such as statins.[26] The contribution of lifestyle changes and cholesterol-lowering pharmaceuticals were accounted for above. The inflammatory mechanism may explain *why* these factors influence health, but so far does not suggest an entirely new source of health improvements.

Other researchers argue that the nutritional intake of a pregnant woman affects the later-life health of her child. The idea is termed "programming": The nutritional, hormonal, and metabolic environment created by the mother influences fetal development in ways that are not reversible.[27] In a famous demonstration, children born during a brief Dutch famine at the end of World War II were more likely to develop diabetes in middle age than children born around the same time but not during the famine.[28] Another study shows that babies born in autumn, when fresh fruits and vegetables are available during most of the pregnancy, live about half a year longer than babies born in spring, when such food is less available.[29]

The programming theory does not seem plausible as an explanation for long-term health improvements, however. In the United States, the total nutritional intake of pregnant women, as measured by average birth weight of their babies, has not changed greatly over time.[30] The United States has had high agricultural output for well over a century. Less is known about the composition of the diet of pregnant women, but the magnitude of the longevity differentials found above are not large enough to generate very big improvements in cardiovascular health.

Still other research focuses on the link between the social environment, stress, and cardiovascular disease. Stress is a natural physical reaction; it helped our ancestors outrun or fight predators. But long-term stress can lead to health problems, including hypertension, depression, gastrointestinal problems, and other health impairments.[31] Different environments produce different levels of stress. Changes in the social environment may thus influence cardiovascular disease risk.

Several environmental factors may influence stress levels. Researcher Michael Marmot argues that job stress is key. In his famous Whitehall study, Marmot shows that workers in lower job grades have more stressful jobs and this adversely affects their health.[32] Changes in job stress are unlikely to explain the improvement in health over time, however. Although there is no good evidence on this, many people believe that jobs have become more stressful in recent years, not less. This suggests that cardiovascular disease rates would be increasing.

At the level of society as a whole, researcher Richard Wilkinson argues that income inequality is a disease risk. He shows that people living in countries with a more unequal income distribution (such as the United States) die at younger ages than people living in countries with a more equal distribution (such as Sweden); he attributes this to reduced social cohesion.[33] The empirical strength of Wilkinson's results has been challenged by researchers who believe that income inequality is really reflecting other aspects of the social environment.[34] But even leaving this aside, the income inequality explanation cannot explain improvements in health over time. Income inequality in the United States has increased since 1950 and social cohesion has declined, both of which would lead to higher mortality, not lower.[35]

On the whole, therefore, medical advances and lifestyle changes appear to be most important in explaining the improvement in health over time. Still, this is an area in which knowledge is progressing rapidly, and conclusions about the importance of these other hypotheses could change in the next few years.

Has medical treatment for cardiovascular disease been worth the cost? The treatments are certainly expensive. In 1950 there was almost no spending on cardiovascular disease. Today, the typical 45-year-old can expect to spend about $30,000 in present value on cardiovascular disease over his or her remaining life.

The benefits of this spending are increased length and quality of life. Quality of life is very difficult to measure over the long term;[36] I thus stick with longevity. The average 45-year-old can expect to live four and a half years longer than he or she could have in 1950, almost entirely because cardiovascular disease mortality has declined.[37] Based on the analysis above, roughly two-thirds of this, or about three years, results from medical treatment changes. Following the earlier analysis, I value these years at $100,000 a year to the person affected and to his or her family, less the cost of keeping people alive in nonworking years. I estimate this cost at $10,000 per year.

Multiplying the additional years by this amount and expressing the results in today's dollars yields a value for medical treatment changes of about $120,000. This is substantially greater than the cost. For every dollar spent, we have realized a return of $4. Once again, the return is sufficiently large to outweigh the uncertainties that are inherent in this calculation. Even if the value of a year of life were only one-quarter as high as I have estimated, cardiovascular disease care would still be worth the cost.

Medical advance, although of a different kind, is also important in explaining lifestyle changes. A large share of behavioral change is attributable to new medical knowledge about disease risk. The decline of cigarette smoking is the clearest example of this.[38] Consumption of cigarettes rose virtually continuously from 1900 to 1960. After the Surgeon General's 1964 report on smoking, however, the number of cigarettes smoked began a steady decline. Today, it is half what it was in 1960. The same is true with dietary changes. Concern about the fat and cholesterol in food, and subsequent changes in food intake, mirror scientific information about the dangers of high cholesterol.

The information that led to these changes can be valued using the same approach as for new pills or surgeries—by considering its costs and benefits. To a significant extent, research into basic medical knowledge is publicly financed, through the National Institutes of Health (NIH). The NIH spends about $10 per person per year on cardiovascular disease research. Much of this spending is not for basic disease knowledge—it is for bench science and clinical trials. Even taking the entire amount, the total cost is about $500 over a person's lifetime. Getting the word out costs money too, perhaps another $500 or so to disseminate information to the public and to have physicians counsel patients.[39] All told, researching and disseminating behavioral information costs perhaps $1,000 per person.

I estimated above that behavioral change accounts for between 10 and 33 percent of lower cardiovascular disease mortality. Using the lower estimate, behavioral change adds about half a year to life expectancy. Valuing this half year at its quality-adjusted value[40] yields $7,000 of benefits. Using the higher estimate gives a value of about $30,000. Compared to the $1,000 cost, the return is thus between 7 and 30 times more. This is astronomical. Indeed, even these returns underestimate the value of behavioral knowledge, because the costs do not need to be repeated for people in other countries or future generations. But there is no sense in going overboard.

People value their health highly. Innovations that improve health, or allow people to extend their lives, thus have very high payoffs.

For medical care to be effective, people must be able to afford it. The issue of affordability is clearly a concern of the uninsured, who rely on the largesse of the medical system as a whole. A large body of literature has examined how cardiovascular-disease-care for the uninsured compares to care for the insured. The conclusions are not reassuring. Uninsured people are less likely to receive hypertension or cholesterol screening than are the insured, are less likely to take medications to control these and other conditions, and are more likely to experience acute diseases.[41]

When acute events occur, the uninsured receive intensive surgical procedures such as bypass surgery and angioplasty less frequently,

and are not transferred as often to hospitals that have those procedures if the initial hospital of admission does not. The uninsured
experience significantly higher mortality in the aftermath.[42]

These poorer outcomes for the uninsured occur even with the
current safety net—emergency rooms that are open to the uninsured
and doctors willing to devote time to them. These efforts help, but
they are not enough to offset the inherent barriers of being without
insurance.

Even among the insured, the fact that medical advances in cardiovascular disease care have been worth it overall does not mean that
all of the money is well spent, or that the medical system does all
that it can. Examined closely, there are multiple errors in cardiovascular disease care: Some individuals get care that is not necessary,
and many go without care that is well worth providing.

First consider the excessive use of care. Evidence of overused care
is most apparent in comparisons of the United States and Canada.
The Canadian government imposes tight limits on the number of
intensive surgical procedures that can be provided. In all of Ontario,
for example, the government allows fewer than ten open-heart surgery units to be in operation. California, by contrast, has three times
the population of Ontario but ten times the number of bypass surgery facilities.

With such limited availability, there is simply no way that Canadian physicians can treat patients as intensively as their American
counterparts do. Canadian doctors wind up prioritizing patients, deciding which should receive intensive surgical therapy and which
should not. As a result, a typical heart attack patient is many times
more likely to get bypass surgery or angioplasty in the United States
than in Canada.[43] And yet, survival after a heart attack is virtually
identical in the two countries.[44] Not everyone in the United States
needs such intensive care. Canada effectively limits care to those for
whom the need is greatest.[45]

Direct evidence on the characteristics of patients who receive
high-tech cardiovascular care also shows that intensive care is frequently overused. Researcher Robert Brook estimates that 15 per-

cent of people who receive cardiac catheterization do not have medical characteristics that make that therapy appropriate.[46] The same is true in about 5 percent of angioplasty cases and 10 percent of bypass surgery cases. We do not need to spend all that we do to get the outcomes we have achieved.

In other cases, care is appropriate but is provided in hospitals that are not very experienced with the procedure, or by physicians who are not the best qualified. Medicine is just like any other field: Practice makes perfect. Hospitals and surgeons that do more bypass surgeries provide better care than hospitals and surgeons that do fewer. A hospital that does at least five hundred bypass surgeries per year, for example, has half the mortality rate of a hospital that does fewer than one hundred.

One would like to see most care provided in these high-volume hospitals, but it doesn't always work that way. In California, for example, two-thirds of bypass surgeries are performed in hospitals that do fewer than five hundred operations per year; one-third are treated in hospitals that do fewer than the minimum number recommended by the American College of Cardiology.[47] Mortality is much higher than it needs to be.

Eliminating open-heart surgery at low-volume hospitals in the United States would not substantially increase the distance to a hospital with that capability. Nor would it cause a wait. Plenty of hospitals in crowded urban areas have a low bypass surgery volume. Ethics is not the explanation here; money is, as I will discuss later.

The most important problem in cardiovascular disease care is not care that is overused or provided in the wrong settings. Rather, it is care that is valuable but is not provided; researchers call this "underuse of care." While we have made great strides in hypertension control in the past 50 years, even today only a quarter of hypertensive patients have their blood pressure at recommended levels; three in four hypertensive patients are at higher risk than they need to be.[48] Fewer than half of diabetics have controlled blood sugar, and rates of cholesterol control are similarly low.[49] On the lifestyle end, many smokers want to quit, but cannot. And more people are obese, even though they search repeatedly for ways to lose weight. Chronic disease management is extremely poor, often with fatal consequences.

There are many causes of underused care—physicians who do not prescribe the right drugs, patients who do not take recommended medications, and so on. One could think about addressing each of these problems individually. But there is a common denominator, I shall argue below, and that is money. There is no money to be made in making sure the right drugs are prescribed or in ensuring that patients take those medications. Indeed, the system discourages this outreach activity by reducing the income of providers when they do it and possibly exposing them to years of litigation. Individuals make mistakes, but the system does not help. We will never get very good care until we change the system as a whole.

What can analysis of cardiovascular disease, infant mortality, and mental illness tell us about the medical system as a whole? A story offers some caution. As babies grow, they get taller and fuller; their head and limb circumference increases along with their length. A friend of mine once determined that if his son, age two at the time, kept growing at the rate he had been for the past year, his son's head would be as big as the moon by the time he reached maturity. That calculation was made about five years ago. The boy is a good size, but I dare say he still fits through a doorway.

My friend's calculation illustrates the difficulty of extrapolating from a sample. Age two is a time when children are growing particularly rapidly. By focusing on growth at this age, my friend was guaranteed to overestimate his son's final size. Extrapolating is a danger in research too. We have seen how the medical system works for infant mortality, mental illness, and cardiovascular disease. If these conditions were typical of medical care writ large, one might be able to say with certainty that medical care was worth the cost. But these conditions are not typical. Death from cardiovascular disease as well as infant mortality have both decreased particularly dramatically in the past half century. To understand the medical system as a whole, we need to know about a wider range of medical conditions. I have not analyzed more conditions, so I cannot go into more detail. In the next chapter, though, I discuss what we can say about the medical system as a whole.

6

MEDICAL CARE:
OF WHAT VALUE?

THE STUDIES OF THE MEDICAL SYS-
tem presented to this point offer several lessons. In each case, spending more over time was worth it. We put more money into the system
than we used to, but we get a lot more in return. But in each case,
the system falls short of its potential. The fate of the uninsured is
particularly problematic. For the mentally ill and people with cardiovascular disease, being uninsured imposes substantial burdens. Care
is received later than is optimal, and is not up to standards for the
insured. The health of the uninsured suffers.

Even among the insured, there are major failures. Some people
receive more care than is appropriate. Others get the right care,
but receive it from providers who are not sufficiently experienced.
Still others get too little care, especially in the management of
chronic disease. Depending on one's perspective, the medical system
either provides enormous benefits (delivering services that vastly ex-
ceed the cost) or is a major embarrassment (failing to do all that it
could).

The primary issue raised by these studies is whether the conclusions are true more generally. While we are not able to answer this
question as definitively as for the case studies, it is almost certain
that these examples are representative of the system as a whole. Let
me explain why.

Consider first the value of spending increases. Is it worth it to spend on health over time? Deciding whether medical spending increases are worth the cost is perhaps the central issue we face in forming health policy. Many health care analysts believe that the rate of cost increase is too high, and that we should restrict subsequent growth. This is made most explicit in so-called "single-payer" proposals. Single-payer proponents want a government-run medical system, as in Canada and as with Medicare in the United States. The government would collect revenues dedicated for health care, and would pay for the care that people received. To ensure the system was affordable over time, the government would restrict the increase in medical costs to no more than the increase in national income—roughly equivalent to the increase in tax revenues. The Clinton health plan had the same feature, although it was not a single-payer proposal. Limits on medical spending increases in the Clinton plan were designed to free up money to pay for covering the uninsured.

In each of these cases, the premise is that increases in medical spending are not providing services of sufficient value to justify what we spend. If this is not true, the premise of these types of proposals is fundamentally unsound.

Medical spending as a whole can be valued using the approach outlined here—weighing the costs and benefits of additional medical inputs. Spending is relatively easy to determine; we know what we spend on medical care and where it goes. The benefits are harder to calculate, however. We know how much longer people live than they used to, but we don't know a lot about quality of life. Further, it is not known how much of mortality reduction in the past half century has resulted from medical advance as opposed to factors such as lifestyle changes, public health improvements, or environmental cleanup. Thus, we cannot perform this calculation explicitly.

Even without specific data, though, we can draw some conclusions. In particular, it is almost certainly the case that increases in medical spending have been worth it. To understand why, consider the longevity gains from medical treatment of low-birth-weight infants and cardiovascular disease patients. We are certain about those gains. If the benefits of medical advance for these two conditions are at least as great as the *entire* increase in medical care spending over time, the medical sector as a whole is bound to be worth it. The only way it could not be worth it would be if all the rest of medical care put together reduced health, which is obviously not the case (as the depression example shows).

I have done this calculation, and it shows that medical care as a whole is worth the cost. As a result of medical improvements for low-birth-weight infants and cardiovascular disease patients, the typical baby born today will live about three and a half years longer than she would have in 1950. To put this in perspective, the entire increase in longevity over this time is about nine years. Medical treatments for these two conditions, therefore, explain more than 40 percent of total longevity improvements. Valuing these years using the approach in the previous chapters yields a value for this medical advance of $50,000 per person.

Fifty thousand dollars is about equal to the increase in medical spending over the typical baby's life. That includes spending on infant care, cardiovascular disease, and everything in between. On the basis of low-birth-weight-infant- and cardiovascular-disease-care alone, therefore, the benefits of medical care are about equal to the costs. Adding in benefits for other conditions would tilt the balance in a favorable direction. It is this conclusion that makes single-payer health reform proposals least attractive.

The high benefit of care is a good feature of the medical system. The status of the uninsured is the biggest problem. Health insurance is the pass key to the medical system. People who lack insurance can't even get in the front door.

About 15 percent of the population, more than 40 million people, is uninsured. The bulk of this group is lower-middle and working class. The very poor receive coverage through public programs, while the better off have private insurance.

A variety of factors lead people to be uninsured. For some, the problem is purely financial. A typical health insurance policy costs about $8,000 for a family and $3,000 for an individual.[1] For a family with an income of even $25,000, this is a substantial amount. In other cases, money is not an absolute constraint so much as one factor among many. A freshly minted, single college graduate earning $30,000 can afford $3,000 for health insurance coverage, but many choose not to take it. While many families with incomes between $30,000 and $50,000 are uninsured, a large share have insurance. Something beyond inability to pay is at work for many.

The other factor is desire. Some people have the (often incorrect) view that they are healthy enough not to need insurance. Other people know there is a safety net available to the uninsured, and choose to rely on that. Being uninsured is not a guarantee of receiving good care but when insurance is expensive, the uninsured option is that much more attractive. Families go without, knowing that they will receive inferior care but assuming it will be adequate. We ran across this phenomenon earlier in explaining why Medicaid expansions for pregnant women cost more than was anticipated. It was noted in that case that many women substituted public coverage for private coverage as Medicaid became more generous. Here, people substitute being uninsured for being insured.[2]

As medical costs have increased, the uninsurance problem has become more severe. In the 1990s, the share of the population that was uninsured rose, despite tremendous economic growth and record job creation. The reason was that families chose to go without coverage as costs increased.[3]

The moral compass of the medical sector is sufficiently strong that the uninsured do not go entirely without. They use emergency rooms when very sick, and public clinics and some private doctors in non-emergency settings. The generosity of the medical system to those without coverage is laudable; such generosity is not found in the provision of other necessities, such as food and shelter.

Still, the efforts of the medical system are not enough to offset the consequences of being uninsured. The evidence on cardiovascular disease and mental illness, discussed above, paints a bleak picture. The same is true for other conditions. A review conducted by the Institute of Medicine found overwhelming evidence of poorer care for the uninsured:[4] The uninsured are significantly less likely to receive prevention and screening services than the insured; serious diseases are detected at a later stage for the uninsured than for the

insured; and uninsured people who have chronic diseases are significantly less likely to have their health conditions appropriately
managed. For example, uninsured people with cancer are diagnosed
at later stages of the disease, receive less intensive therapy, and have
a higher mortality rate as a result.[5]

Overall, the Institute of Medicine estimates that about 20,000 non-
elderly adults die each year because they are uninsured.[6] That is
equal to the total number of deaths from diabetes and strokes in
that age group.

Using the framework that has been presented, we can evaluate
whether or not the benefits of universal insurance coverage justify
the costs. Extending coverage to the uninsured would cost about $20
billion per year.[7] This amount covers the medical services the uninsured would use if insured; it is not the amount the government
would have to pay to insure the uninsured. The governmental costs
of universal coverage are much higher, since many uninsured have
incomes similar to people who have insurance, and the government
would have to provide equal subsidies to everyone in an income
range—even those already having insurance. I discuss the public-
sector costs of universal insurance coverage later. In evaluating
whether it would be good for society to extend coverage to the uninsured, however, the net increase in medical spending is the appropriate cost to consider, not the transfers from one payer to another.

Among the benefits of insuring the uninsured are the additional
years of life and increased quality of life the uninsured would experience. Based on the age distribution of people without insurance and
the value of a year of life, the benefits of reduced mortality alone
would be about $33 billion. There would presumably be quality-of-life
improvements as well, but these are more difficult to measure.

The productivity effects of insuring the uninsured would be small.
The uninsured would work more at younger ages but collect more
in Social Security and Medicare when retired. Over their life as a
whole, people collect in benefits about what they pay in taxes, so the
productivity effects of reducing mortality for the uninsured is near
zero.

Comparing the costs and benefits shows that extending insurance coverage to the uninsured would be a good social investment. For every dollar spent, the benefits would be about $1.50. There is thus an economic, as well as moral, case for universal insurance coverage.

This social calculation masks large variations in the costs and benefits to different people. Enacting universal insurance coverage would allow the uninsured to live longer, healthier lives, but much of the bill is likely to be paid by those who are already insured. There is no way to escape the fact that providing insurance to everyone requires transferring resources from those on a higher rung to those in the middle and bottom of the income distribution. Such transfers take place now, albeit in a roundabout way. Higher-income people pay higher insurance premiums to cover uncompensated care to the poor, and they pay taxes for programs used disproportionately by the poor. But enacting universal coverage will increase the required transfers. These transfers will have to come from the government.

In the past, the need for these transfer has been a major impediment to reform. In the early 1990s, for example, conventional forecasts suggested that the government could not support universal insurance coverage without major cutbacks in other activities. The booming economy of the late 1990s changed that conclusion, however. Rapid economic growth led to significant income increase and correspondingly higher government revenues. Of course, economies go through up years and down years, and money is less available in the down years than in the up. But the issues in insurance coverage is not the vicissitudes of economic cycles, but designing policies that make sense over the good and bad together. It was clear early in the twenty-first century that we had enough money to support coverage at this level when not in a recession.

What has changed since then is the major tax reductions of the Bush administration. In 2001 and 2003, the Bush administration used most of those additional revenues for tax cuts targeted at the very wealthy. That was a mistake; by reorienting those tax cuts to the population as a whole, we could have secured universal insurance coverage without raising taxes. I present more details in Chapter 10.

The problems of the medical system are not limited to the uninsured. The case studies also highlighted enormous failures in treatment of the insured—people using too many services, receiving care at low-volume hospitals or by inexperienced physicians, or not receiving enough care. Sadly this is also true about the medical system as a whole.

Consider first the care that is overused. We encountered this in many settings: people using antidepressants who don't need them, and doctors performing intensive cardiovascular procedures when they are not appropriate. This type of overuse occurs frequently. Most commonly, overuse is found in intensive settings—invasive surgeries, sophisticated diagnostic techniques, and the like. Acute care is commonly overused; less acute care is not. To presage the upcoming analysis, services that are reimbursed very generously are overused, while services that are reimbursed less well are not.

Researcher Jack Wennberg and colleagues at Dartmouth have documented the enormous amount of overused care. These researchers study Medicare costs in different areas of the country, showing large variation across areas. Residents of Miami, for example, use twice as many Medicare services as people living in Minneapolis. Areas that spend more on medical care, however, do not seem to have significantly better health outcomes.[8]

The Wennberg analysis suggests that about 20 percent of Medicare spending could be eliminated with no adverse effects on health.[9] In the medical system as a whole, a 20 percent savings (assuming the same waste as in Medicare) translates into $1,000 per person, a very large amount.

———————

Use of care in low-volume hospitals or by physicians who are not adequately trained is part of a general class of mistakes termed "misuse of care"—the application of care that is appropriate, but not provided at the right time or in the right way. Substantial evidence points to large amounts of misused care.

Operating at low-volume hospitals is just the tip of the iceberg in terms of misused care. Misuse of pharmaceuticals has been investigated most extensively. The health reporter for the *Boston Globe* died a few years ago when she was given the wrong dosage of chemotherapy for breast cancer. The attending physician made a calculation error that was not caught by the pharmacist (he forgot to divide the total dosage into four daily doses). The reporter overdosed and died. Beyond this sort of tragic mistake, people are sometimes given drugs to which they are allergic, drugs that adversely interact with other medications they are taking, and drugs in the wrong dosages.

One is tempted to blame doctors for these errors, and they do deserve some blame. But what is more striking is the fact that the system is not set up to catch errors. For example, computers can easily catch incorrect dosages. So-called computerized physician order entry systems exist and are very effective.[10] Yet use of computer-aided prescription technology is depressingly low. We rely on medical personnel to be infallible when no one can be.

The overall loss from this failure is enormous. The Institute of Medicine estimates that about 50,000 to 100,000 people die each year because of medical errors occurring in hospitals, making medical errors one of the leading causes of death.[11]

Perhaps the most important failure occurs when people do not get enough care, termed underuse of care. We saw examples of this too: depressed people who are not diagnosed or given appropriate medications; hypertension or high cholesterol that is not controlled; and pregnant women who receive no help quitting smoking. Across the spectrum of medical care, poor disease management is far more common than is good management.[12]

Consider a specific example, the use of beta-blockers in people who have had a heart attack. Almost all people who have survived a heart attack should take beta-blockers; these drugs reduce the workload of the heart and cut the probability of a recurrent heart attack by about one-quarter.[13] But studies show that only half of patients who are candidates for a beta-blocker receive a prescription for one.[14] At the patient end, only half of those who are given a prescription for a beta-blocker are on the medication several months later. In total, therefore, only one-quarter of heart attack survivors regularly take these lifesaving medications.[15]

Lack of insurance is not the major issue here; the studies of beta-blocker underuse are done on the insured. Nor is managed care the culprit; beta-blocker use is as low or lower in Medicare than in managed care. And fans of the Canadian single-payer system should know that virtually the same share of people with a heart attack fail to receive beta-blockers in Canada as in the United States.[16] Undertreatment of chronic disease is a pervasive part of all medical systems, not an isolated error in one corner.

One thinks first of assessing blame. One reason that physicians do not write prescriptions for beta-blockers is that they are not up on the latest literature; specialists in cardiovascular medicine prescribe beta-blockers more than generalists.[17] Certainly, physicians should stay on top of the medical literature. But there are more than ten thousand clinical trials conducted annually.[18] Physicians are no more capable of processing them all than are the rest of us.

Rather than relying on physicians to know everything, we should imagine instead alternative structures. For example, computers could be used to help doctors with diagnosis and prescriptions, spotting patients who were not prescribed appropriate medications. In addition, physicians could work in teams rather than individually. Teamwork would take advantage of complementary knowledge among physicians with different expertise cardiologists and general practitioners, for example. Neither of these solutions is regularly employed, however. As a result, the mistakes persist.

At the patient level, one notices how unfriendly the medical system is. Physician appointments can take several weeks to schedule, and often require missing work. Medication side effects or other follow-up needs require further visits. There are trips to the pharmacist and testing offices. If a person slips up, his treatment suffers.

Contrast this with the way we interact with other industries. People can phone the bank at any hour of the day, but not their doctor's office. We can arrange for book or clothes delivery over the Internet; and we can get a pizza delivered in about half an hour, but not a monthly prescription. Computers remind us to pay bills, but not to take prescriptions. Priests are online but few doctors are.[19] Veterinarians send out annual reminders to bring the dog in for a visit, but primary care physicians do not send such reminders for us. The health care system is far more difficult to use than most other industries, and the system's performance suffers.

Lifestyle changes are even more problematic. People become ill in part because they eat too much, exercise too little, and smoke cigarettes. Almost everyone knows that these behaviors are harmful; the difficulty people have is in changing what they do. In practice, though, the medical system does very little to help people change their behaviors, other than lecturing them about the need to do so. If lifestyle changes were just a question of knowledge, people would have made them already. There are other things at work. As we saw with pregnant women, some interventions lead to smoking cessation, particularly those that involve regular follow-up and feedback. But these interventions are almost never made.

Managing chronic disease successfully is like running a hurdle race. To succeed, one has to leap over a series of hurdles. Independently, each hurdle is minor. Together, they add up to a major barrier. People need help clearing all the hurdles.

Solving the underuse problem will require restructuring the medical system. It will also cost money, at least in the short run. People need to be seen by doctors, tested, and given medications. But the money would clearly be worth it; the therapies that are underused are almost all relatively inexpensive and quite valuable.

No one has attempted to compile an overall estimate of how much more we would spend by filling in the underuse of care. My guess is that we could easily spend several hundred dollars more per person on medical care, below the $1,000 per person of overused care, but still a significant sum.

———————

Imagine, for a moment, that the uninsured could be insured, underused care provided, and overused care eliminated. There is no magic wand with which to do this, but I will present some ideas in Chapters 9 and 10. What would the medical system look like then?

Eliminating overused care and providing more care when underused have offsetting effects on medical spending. The first saves money; the second costs. We do not know which amount is larger, but the calculations above suggest they are about the same size. That means that a better medical care system would not spend much less than the one we currently have.

Over time, medical spending could well increase, as a result of the continued development of new technologies. Many technologies induce more people to be treated who formerly were not, which adds to total costs. As we saw, SSRIs are an example of this. In some cases, new technologies replace more expensive existing treatments and thus save money, but this is rare.[20]

The prospect that medical innovation will drive up medical spending even more raises enormous concerns. Can we afford to spend more than we do now? Will it be bad for the economy? Richard Lamm, the former governor of Colorado, has been most outspoken about the need to limit access to medical care: "We simply have invented and discovered more things to do to our aging bodies than our aging society can afford to pay for. We are on the threshold of the bionic body where medicine can have some positive impact on practically every organ in our body. We have created a Faustian bargain where our aging bodies can and will divert resources that our children and grandchildren need for their own families and that public policy needs for other important social goods. . . . Do we really know what we are doing to our society and its institutions? What does it mean to our nation's future?"[21] Lamm's comments follow a line dating back as far as the Greek playwright Euripides, who wrote nearly 2,500 years ago:

> I hate the men who would prolong their lives
> By foods and drinks and charms of magic art
> Perverting nature's course to keep off death
> They ought, when they no longer serve the land
> To quit this life, and clear the way for youth.

In contrast to these pessimistic views, I believe that we can afford additional medical spending, and further that it will be good for us as a society to do so. Let me explain.

A first concern is what we have to look forward to as a result of spending more. Obviously, we do not know exactly what increased medical spending will buy. But we can make some guesses. The single most important technological development in medicine is likely to be the understanding of the human genome.[22] The genome refers to the 30,000 to 40,000 human genes found in the nucleus of each human cell. Genes code for proteins, which drive the body's functions: regulating when cells are born and die, where energy is stored, and how disease is fought. People with genetic abnormalities have a higher (or sometimes lower) predisposition to disease.

A working draft of the human genome has already been produced. That draft is being refined, and scientists are starting the transition to understanding what the genome means.[23] One benefit of this knowledge will be earlier detection of disease. For example, scientists recently discovered that women with abnormalities in genes known as BRCA1 and BRCA2 are at increased risk of breast and ovarian cancer. Women with these abnormalities are less able to repair damage to DNA than are women without the abnormalities. BRCA abnormalities can be screened for at any age. Thus, young women can know if they are at elevated risk for breast cancer well before any such cancer has occurred. Women at high risk can have more frequent mammograms and breast screenings, can avoid risky behaviors such as weight gain and hormone replacement therapy, and in the extreme can have prophylactic mastectomy or chemotherapy.

Genetic knowledge may also lead to new therapies. Defective genes cannot currently be replaced, although this may be possible down the road.[24] More important in the short term is the development of new therapies based on genetic knowledge. The recent approval of the drug Gleevec for the treatment of chronic myeloid leukemia (CML) is an example of this. CML is a disease in which the body produces excess quantities of immature white blood cells, which circulate in the blood and drive out mature red blood cells. Without enough red blood cells, the internal organs will not get enough oxygen and will die. CML is a painful, usually fatal disease. Prior to Gleevec, the only long-term solution for patients with CML was bone marrow transplantation, an extremely difficult and not very effective treatment.

Genetic analysis led to a new therapy, however. Examination of the DNA of patients with CML showed that the disease resulted from an exchange of genetic material on two chromosomes, leading the body to produce an altered protein that stimulates excessive white blood cell production. Gleevec was engineered to inhibit the action of the defective gene. It prevents the formation of excessive white blood cells, with few side effects. To date, Gleevec has been extremely successful.

The reduction in drug side effects is important in other cases too. Patients with CML are willing to go through very painful treatments to try to beat the disease. But that is not true of people with all conditions. One of the causes of underuse of care in many settings is the side effects from therapy. Knowing more about which drugs produce which side effects—likely influenced by genetic differences across people—will allow physicians to target particular therapies to different people.

Genetic knowledge is only one area in which medicine is likely to improve; there are other areas as well. A few years ago, research findings suggested a possible new way to treat cancer. Researcher Judah Folkman at Children's Hospital in Boston noted that cancerous tumors need a supply of oxygen to grow. If the tumor could be prevented from developing blood vessels, its growth would be inhibited. The result has been a wealth of research on new ways to prevent tumor growth. This research may or may not bear fruit, but it illustrates the range of possibilities.

Diagnostic imaging, such as mammography, is likely to improve as well. Even with today's technology, it is difficult to spot very small cancers on an X-ray. Improved imaging devices in the future could improve the screening process, allowing screening at younger ages, earlier cancer detection, and more effective treatment.

Most of these therapies are likely to increase costs—they are expensive and are used in people who currently get little care. The research money spent to date—measured in the billions—is small compared to the ultimate cost of treatment. But the advances will improve health.

Even if we develop new ways of bringing about major health gains, is medical care really the right place to spend our money? We have to give up some things to afford more care, and the things we give up have value too. In the health economics lingo, this is termed the "sustainability" debate—can we sustain medical spending increases at their current rate, valuable as they might be?

Sustainability has been a long-standing concern of policymakers.[25] Some years ago, it was common to believe that medical care would not be affordable if it reached 10 percent of GDP. That number was reached and surpassed without any catastrophe. But as the numbers continue to grow, the concerns become more acute. The typical family in the United States earns about $35,000 annually, of which about $5,000 goes to medical care (including direct payments, employer-based payments, and taxes to pay for public programs). Projections are that medical spending will increase to one-quarter of income by mid-century, $9,000 for a family today.[26] Is that too much?

While that amount seems clearly excessive, there is a good reason not to worry: People in the future will earn more than people do today, and that will make their spending burden smaller. Compared to the $35,000 now earned, the typical family earned perhaps $30,000 a decade ago. The same family is expected to earn nearly $75,000 by mid-century. Even if medical care took one-quarter of that amount (nearly $19,000), nonmedical consumption would still be large. In fact, it would be significantly greater than today.

In the classic analogy, think of total income as a pie. The size of the economic pie is expanding over time, with improvements in productivity. At the same time, the medical care slice is growing. In the race between the two, the pie is expanding sufficiently rapidly that the nonmedical care part is still increasing.

The trade-off we face is that if we have more rapid medical spending, we get slower increases of everything else—new cars bought less frequently, less frequent updating of new computers, houses being built with a longer delay, and so on. People have different views about whether that is reasonable, but I see no reason that this trade-off cannot be made.

The typical American family will continue to be able to afford increased medical spending, but not all families will. Those at the bottom of the income ladder will find it increasingly difficult to afford the increases in medical care costs if their incomes stagnate. That is what has happened in the past few decades, as insurance coverage has declined among those in the bottom of the distribution.

If we want everyone to benefit from medical progress, we have to make sure that all can afford the cost. In practice, that means that government will have to help those at the bottom of the ladder afford insurance. Within existing government budgets, providing additional support is barely feasible. Beyond medical care, the vast bulk of government spending goes for a few basic services: defense, Social Security, interest payments, and education. If government revenues do not rise, we will have to pay for increased medical care by squeezing out these valuable services. (We could run deficits for a while, but deficits must ultimately be paid back. At the point of payback, services would have to be cut.) These services really cannot be cut that much. The only solution is to transfer some of the increasing economic pie to government, perhaps in the form of a dedicated health insurance revenue stream.

There is precedent for such a step. A century ago, our government was a shadow of its current self. Government provided national defense (at a much smaller level), built roads and sewers, and organized police and fire protection. Today, public revenues are ten times greater. Most of the new money goes to programs, such as Social Security, Medicare, and Medicaid, that we wanted to provide but that only government can. If we want to expand government's responsibility, we will need to pay for it.

Fundamentally, the problem of medical costs is not one of affordability. We can afford to spend more on medical care if we want to. The real problem is value. We have a medical system that is valuable, but not as valuable as it could be. Medical care reform needs to address the value question more than the affordability question.

7

YOU GET WHAT YOU PAY FOR

"Money makes the world go 'round," or so it is said, and medical care is no exception. Even the noblest doctor or most public-spirited hospital cannot provide medical services for free. The way the money flows thus influences what is done. To see why the medical system does what it does, therefore, we need to follow the flow of dollars.

Money is clearly important in explaining why some people are uninsured, as discussed previously. Somewhat more complex, however, is the situation of the insured. As we have seen, having insurance—even very generous insurance—does not always translate into receiving good care. Why does the system fail so frequently? Understanding this issue requires us to delve into the history of medical care and the payment for medical services.[1]

Early in the twentieth century, there were few well-trained doctors, and little that doctors could do to help their patients. Doctors made house calls because all the tools they needed could fit in a little black bag. This limited ability to treat people kept the cost of medical care low. Medical spending early in the twentieth century was less than a tenth of what it is today and was not increasing over time.

Low spending, in turn, limited the demand for health insurance. The goal of insurance, after all, is to spread money from the healthy to the sick. If being sick isn't that costly, there is not much need for insurance. Most insurance at the time covered lost wages when people were sick, not medical costs.[2]

The first insurance companies were not set up until the late 1920s. Originally, they were operated by providers. Providers felt some obligation to care for people when they were sick, even if they didn't have much money. Getting people to prepay for care when they were healthy increased the certainty of payment. The first medical insurance company, Blue Cross, began offering hospital insurance in 1929 and Blue Shield started to offer insurance for physician care a few years later. The two companies subsequently merged. Medical care was cheap: The first Blue Cross plan charged patients a monthly fee of $.50 (about $5 today) in exchange for up to three weeks of hospital care per year if needed. Today, a typical plan for an individual costs about $200 per month.[3]

Over time, better knowledge of disease and physicians' expanding technical capabilities increased the value of medical care. World War II and its aftermath were the time of biggest change. Penicillin and sulfa drugs were discovered and were shown to have magical effects in curing infections. They became widely available in the late 1940s. Surgery and mental health care both improved during the war. As life settled down with the return of peace, people wanted access to these new types of care.

Demand for medical care translated into demand for health insurance. The post-World War II era saw a boom in health insurance enrollment. Blue Cross/Blue Shield policies multiplied, and commercial insurance companies, seeing the expanding business, entered the field as well.

Government policy strongly influenced the way that people got health insurance. During World War II, the federal government limited the wages that firms could pay, in an effort to limit inflation. An exception was made for health insurance, however, which was deemed to be a benefit, not a wage payment. Firms competing for labor thus began to provide health insurance to their workers.

After World War II, wage controls were eliminated, but tax policy encouraged employers to provide insurance. The IRS ruled in the early 1950s that employer payments for health insurance were not to be counted as personal income for tax purposes. Thus, money that employers contributed to health insurance was not taxed, while wage payments to employees were, even if subsequently used to buy health insurance. This effectively provided a big subsidy to employer-provided health insurance. The result was a major increase in employer provision of health insurance.

As commercial insurers entered the health care business, they needed to decide the details of policies. People running these companies did not know what services were necessary or what doctors should be paid for care. How could they decide what to pay? The simplest decision is to let doctors and patients decide what is needed and how much should be charged for the services. Doctors are the experts in medical care, after all. They should make the medical decisions.

At the limit, this argues for full reimbursement of all medical care received. That clearly was not practical; patients needed to pay some of the cost of care, so that they didn't overuse services. But the patient costs should not be excessive.

In economic parlance, the overuse of medical services resulting from people being shielded from the true costs of care is termed "moral hazard." Insurance actuaries once used the term to connote a moral failure on the part of people buying insurance (they did not control what they did when insured). Now, the term simply refers to the fact that people use more services when the price of care is lower.

The concept of moral hazard, if not the terminology, goes back to Adam Smith, who in 1776 wrote about corporate directors: "The directors of such companies, however, being the managers rather of other peoples' money than of their own, it cannot well be expected, that they should watch over it with the same anxious vigilance with which the partners in a private copartnery frequently watch over their own. . . . Negligence and profusion, therefore, must always prevail, more or less, in the management of the affairs of such a company."[4] A more amusing depiction was provided by the famous playwright George Bernard Shaw nearly a century ago: "That any sane nation, having observed that you could provide for the supply of bread by giving bakers a pecuniary interest in baking for you, should go on to give a surgeon a pecuniary interest in cutting off your leg, is enough to make one despair of political humanity."[5] We do not cut off legs so readily (perhaps) but we do operate on other parts of the body in situations in which it is not always needed.

The policies that insurers developed in the 1950s and 1960s reflected a balance between the desire to limit moral hazard and the goal not to have people exposed to too much risk. A typical insurance plan required the enrollee to pay the first $500 or so of care out of pocket, and then 20 percent of costs above that amount, up to a maximum payment of perhaps $1,500. For small expenses, these cost-sharing amounts were significant; to avoid paying for the full cost of care themselves, many people did not go for routine visits. In the case of more serious illnesses, however, the cost-sharing provisions rarely had much effect. A patient with a serious injury rapidly exceeded the maximum patient payment, and thus did not pay a great deal for additional care. That is still true today. "What do I need, doctor?" is heard often. "Can I afford it?" is much rarer.

Rather than using high cost sharing to discourage use, insurers instead simply decided not to cover some services. The first insurance plans covered hospital and physician care only; other services were not sufficiently costly or were too subject to moral hazard. Prescription drug coverage was added in the 1960s and 1970s, as the benefits of pharmaceuticals became apparent and as expensive drugs began to be developed. Medicare was created before coverage for prescription drugs was common, and it has never added that coverage, to the consternation of many elderly. Mental health care, dental care, and prenatal care (in the terminology of the day, "mental, dental, and placental coverage") were added in the 1970s and 1980s.

The first insurers also had to decide how to reimburse providers for the services they rendered. The simplest solution was simply to pay the prices that hospitals and doctors charged. Providers already had prices, after all, just as all firms did. It was easiest for insurers simply to pay those prices. Such a payment system is termed "fee-for-service reimbursement." The predominance of fee-for-service reimbursement was to have a major effect on the development of modern medicine. It came about largely by convenience, not with great forethought.

Ultimately, insurers had to get more involved in pricing issues. As more people became insured in the 1960s and 1970s, doctors and hospitals found that they could charge very high prices, because only the insurer was paying. To counter this, insurers developed elaborate fee schedules. Doctors were paid on the basis of what they charged, up to a limit based on the prices paid to other doctors in the area.[6] The scheme was more complicated, but the theme was the same— reimbursement was on a fee-for-service basis, with doctors determining what was appropriate.

The pure fee-for-service era dates from the 1950s to the early 1990s, when fee-for-service insurance largely (although not totally) gave way to managed care. Still, the fee-for-service system dominated the historical development of medicine and has strong residual effects today. To make sense of the medical system, therefore, we need to understand the operation of that system.

While fee-for-service insurance pays for any medical service provided, in practice the system pays more for high-tech care than for less intensive care, because high-tech care involves more of a physician's time and greater skill. Bypass surgeons make thousands of dollars on each procedure, for example. A physician regularly performing such surgery can net several hundred thousand dollars per year after practice expenses and insurance. With payments so generous, there is no shortage of doctors willing to operate on patients.

Routine care is reimbursed well, but less generously. Fees are reimbursed when patients visit the doctor, but primary care physicians make far less than their interventional brethren. Care provided outside of traditional office settings is not covered at all. Having a nurse call patients to check on medication compliance is not a medical care visit and thus is not reimbursed. E-mail communication never made it into fee-for-service reimbursement and remains unreimbursed today. Error checking is in the same category. Monitoring prescription doses, looking for allergic reactions, and verifying referrals are all uncompensated.

This division of payments by intensity is fundamental to the story, so let me explain it in some detail. We can position medical services along two dimensions: how intensive the care is, and how valuable it is. At the more intensive end are high-tech surgeries, such as bypass surgery and angioplasty. These services are among the most sophisticated that medicine can deliver. Intensive surgeries are valuable in some patients and ineffective in others.

Moderately intensive care includes chronic disease diagnosis and treatment: performing regular mammograms and cholesterol screenings, writing and updating prescriptions as appropriate, and referring patients to specialists at the right times. Providing these services involves a fair amount of physician ability, but these services are not nearly as intensive as invasive surgery. Most of these moderate services are valuable, although some are not.

The least intensive services are follow-up and routine monitoring: providing reminders about medication usage and testing, coordinating patient education materials, and maintaining telephone or e-mail contact. Many of these can be performed by clerical staff. They are valuable, but not very intensive.

The ideal medical care system would encourage services with high value and discourage services with low value. Included in the high-value category are some very intensive services, some moderately intensive services, and some non-intensive services. The fee-for-service system does not provide incentives this way, however. Fee-for-service plans pay on the basis of intensity, not value. Intensive services are strongly encouraged, while less intensive services are neglected.

Adding to the case for doing more is the fact that patients pay little out of pocket for very intensive care, and so have few incentives to limit such care. The clincher is the potential for doctors to be sued if care is not provided and the patient suffers an adverse outcome. Doctors fearing such a situation deliver intensive services whenever there is the slightest doubt. Less intensive services are not as essential, however, and so are not viewed with the same urgency.

As we have seen, the preference for intensive over less intensive care corresponds well to what happened over time. Patients for whom intensive therapy was helpful were well served. A lot was spent on them, but the benefits were even greater. Along with this valuable care, though, came a lot of overuse. There is often a thin line between what is valuable and what is not. When payment is generous, doctors perceive things to be appropriate that they otherwise would not, and thus do them more frequently. Routine management and follow-up services are underprovided, as befits their low rate of reimbursement.

In addition to encouraging the use of technologies that were already available, the fee-for-service payment system created powerful incentives to develop new technologies, particularly very intensive ones. Intensive surgeries or devices that improved health found a wide audience, whether the health improvement was large or modest. This spurred the developers of medical technology to create a steady flow of new innovations. Central as it is to our story, the development of new technologies bears a bit more discussion.

Medical innovations come from many sources—researchers at the lab bench, doctors in clinical practice, and pathologists in laboratories, to name a few. Economically, we can divide these innovations into two groups: those produced by scientists and clinicians without a corporate sponsor, and those produced by for-profit firms. New surgeries are typical examples of the former. Surgeries are not commercial products to be patented and sold. Rather, a technique is developed, described in medical journals, and used freely by all surgeons. New drugs and imaging devices are examples of the latter. They are developed by commercial firms and sold on an exclusive basis for a profit.

Researchers working on noncommercial innovations are typically not motivated by money. Most people do not weather the years of education required for an academic career because they believe they will get rich. Personal motivations are much more important. Many innovations are developed in response to clinicians' seeing patients for whom there is no other treatment. The possibility for international fame also strongly motivates academic researchers.

The major factor driving this type of research is government and hospital support for the research enterprise itself. Clinicians need free time and money to experiment with new therapies. Biomedical researchers need money to pay for labs, equipment, and research assistants. Historically, there were two sources of funding for this research. The first was from the government, in the form of research grants. Since World War II, the U.S. government has made significant commitments to medical research, largely through the National Institutes of Health. The National Institutes of Health spends over $20 billion each year on biomedical research (about $100 per person).

Hospitals are the second source of research funding. Hospitals with a research commitment typically charge more than do non-research institutions. These additional funds are used to support their physicians' research activities. This method of support is on much less solid footing than is public funding. As medical care markets have become tighter, with the expansion of managed care and government payment cutbacks, hospital-based funding of research has plummeted. For the most part, there is little of this internal financing left.

In commercial research, principally that of pharmaceutical companies and medical device manufacturers, the dominant factor driving research is obviously money. The average new drug costs about $500 million to develop, once the costs of testing and the inevitable failures are added in.[7] For firms to be willing to conduct this research, the expected return for developing a new drug has to be high. Generous payment systems allow firms to recoup their initial investment rapidly, and thus spur research into new innovations. The fee-for-service system was a boon to this type of research.

To see the alternative, go far away from the United States—to sub-Saharan Africa. Millions of people in sub-Saharan Africa survive on the equivalent of a dollar a day in income. As one might imagine, health problems in these societies are profound. Every year, five million Africans die of malaria, tuberculosis, and AIDS, about five times the number of deaths from heart disease and cancer combined in the United States.[8]

Experts generally believe that vaccines against some or all of these conditions could be developed, were enough research devoted to the problem. Malaria and tuberculosis in particular are good candidates for vaccines; AIDS might be as well, although its case is less certain.

And yet, pharmaceutical companies devote virtually no money to developing such vaccines. Less than a penny of every dollar of medical research goes to malaria and tuberculosis. More money is spent on potential AIDS vaccines, but essentially all of that research is on the strains of the AIDS-causing virus [or HIV] prevalent in developed countries. It is not at all clear that a vaccine for that strain of AIDS would work against the strain prevalent in Africa.

The reason for the lack of research is simple: money. Poor Africans cannot afford to pay high prices for new medications. Thus, there is no incentive for pharmaceutical companies to develop them. From a business standpoint, these companies are doing exactly what they should. But the outcome is horrible. No money means no research, and no research means more deaths.

Indeed, the situation is getting worse, as we frequently hear from the media. While there is no vaccine for AIDS, recent advances in medications for people with AIDS seem to keep virus levels low. In developed countries, millions of people with AIDS taking these medications are being spared an early death. These new treatment packages are expensive, though, selling for up to $10,000 per patient per year in the United States. That amount is far above production cost, but it allows the pharmaceutical companies to recoup their initial investment in research—and make a profit.

The government of South Africa recently decided that it wanted access to these drugs at a lower cost. In 1997 it passed a law allowing generic versions of AIDS drugs to be imported. Generic drugs are the same as the branded drug, but they are produced by companies copying a competitor's research. Without original research costs to recoup, generic drug makers can charge much less. The pharmaceutical companies, fearing that poor countries might buy generic drugs at low prices and resell them cheaply in rich countries, filed a lawsuit to stop the implementation of the law. The South African government, and Nelson Mandela in particular, were named as defendants.

This may have been a good legal strategy, but it made for horrible publicity. Suing Nelson Mandela for helping poor South Africans spurred protests against the drug companies worldwide. As the trial was about to start, the drug companies could no longer take the bad publicity and dropped the lawsuit. They agreed to sell their AIDS drugs in Africa at production cost, about $600 per patient per year.

The situation in South Africa reinforced a horrible lesson—there is no incentive to develop therapies when the amount for which they can be sold is low. It is virtually inconceivable that the private sector will mount a sustained research effort against the diseases of the poor after this meltdown. Even sadder, the poor in Africa are no better off than they were before. Poor South Africans with AIDS can no more afford $600 per year in treatment costs than $10,000 per year. The result was a fiasco all around.

The United States is in no danger of becoming as stingy as South Africa in its payment for new pharmaceuticals. But the lesson holds. The incentives in payment policy influence what it is profitable to explore. Paying well for medical care led to rapid innovation and its resulting gains. Cutting back would have the opposite effect.

The dynamics of the fee-for-service payment system ultimately led to its demise. Over time, the increase in costs of the traditional system made the payers of medical services nervous. Throughout the 1970s and 1980s, employers providing health insurance found themselves facing continually higher benefit costs. While these costs were ultimately pushed onto workers in the form of lower wages, making this happen was not so easy. Governments found spending on Medicare and Medicaid rising more rapidly than tax revenues to pay for them. Families found their out-of-pocket bills rising as well, even as their cash wages were falling and taxes to pay for public medical programs were going up. Added to this cost concern was the fear of becoming uninsured and being bankrupted by medical bills. As costs increased, this fear grew correspondingly stronger. At the dawn of the 1990s, the stage was set for fundamental reform.

8

THE MANAGED CARE DEBACLE

AT THE START OF THE CLINTON AD-
ministration, it looked like there would be dramatic changes in
health care. People were fed up with the lack of universal coverage
and the rising cost of medical care. President Clinton was elected
with a mandate to reform health care. Businesses and families looked
to government for answers. The Clinton health plan, of course, failed
to garner support. The thud of failure was heard in every family
room and corporate boardroom in America. The federal government was not going to solve the health care problem; the private
sector was on its own.

People could do little about the system by themselves; businesses
could do more. With a common focus unique in recent times, businesses began badgering their insurers for lower costs. How could
they pay less for medical care than they currently paid? The answer
they got was managed care.

Managed care was not new in the 1990s. The first managed care
plans started before World War II, and managed care was widespread in areas of the country such as California and Massachusetts
as early as the 1980s. But the plans in the 1990s were qualitatively
different from those that came before. Ironically, given what we
know today, the first managed care plans were started for idealistic
reasons; doctors thought that delivering care outside the traditional
setting would allow them to practice more preventive care and deal
with their patients in a more humane way. Many patients were ini-

tially attracted to these plans for the same reason. The performance of these early plans, such as Kaiser Permanente in California, Harvard Community Health Plan in Massachusetts, and Group Health Cooperative in Seattle, was reasonably good; they cost less than traditional insurance, and people in those plans were relatively happy. In the 1990s, though, cost savings began to drive managed care more than its founding ideals. Preventive care was fine, but pressure to cut costs was building.

The 1990s saw a stampede into managed care. Employers that had previously offered only traditional insurance policies now offered managed care plans as well. In some cases, traditional insurance policies were eliminated entirely. When the traditional plans were offered, they were very expensive. The change was dramatic. Only 5 percent of the privately insured population was in managed care in 1980. Today, it is 95 percent. Traditional insurance is an anachronism; only Medicare recipients and other small pockets of people (for example, some union workers) have such coverage.

Managed care is a catchphrase for what are actually a number of different types of health insurance organizations. The health maintenance organization, or HMO, is the most well-known form of managed care. HMO plans contract with specific providers and carefully monitor what services those providers perform. But HMOs are only one variety of managed care insurers. There are also preferred provider organizations (PPOs)—a looser network of doctors who agree to accept lower fees in exchange for being in a plan's network, and point of service plans (POSs)—HMOs that allow people to use some services outside the network. The plans vary in their restrictiveness: HMOs are most restrictive and PPOs least. Rather than provide a taxonomy, however, I will consider all the plans together, under the common rubric of managed care. In comparison to the fee-for-service system, the similarities among managed care plans are more notable than the differences.

At heart, managed care is a system in which insurers intensively monitor aspects of the care process. Traditional insurers did not meddle in care decisions. Managed care insurers, in contrast, approve tests and procedures, steer patients to some medications over others, and limit the use of hospitals and other expensive forms of care.

In some cases, managed care insurers place explicit limitations on what doctors can do, such as requiring approval before certain tests or procedures are performed and denying payment for care deemed unnecessary. The direct restrictions are known in the industry as "utilization review"—monitoring utilization to make sure it is not excessive.

A perceived excess of hospital care was the first concern of managed care insurers, who believed that too many people were admitted to hospitals and that they stayed too long. They attacked hospital costs with a vengeance, requiring second opinions before nonemergency admissions, and monitoring length of stay to see where extra days might be trimmed. After rising for decades, hospital costs began a prolonged decline in the 1980s and 1990s. Only in the past few years has the decline leveled off.

Physicians are subject to utilization review as well. Many physicians need to obtain approval before performing routine tests or referring a patient to a specialist. The 800-numbers that doctors complain about having to call for approval are a part of this process.

Financial incentives have reinforced these direct restrictions. Many managed care plans create financial incentives for providers to do less. Primary care physicians, for example, are often paid a fixed sum per patient in their practice. Out of this amount, the physician must pay for all medical services used by the patient—tests, exams, screenings, hospitalizations, and so on. Thus, doctors lose money when they provide additional care. Similar systems are in place at some hospitals.[1]

Finally, managed care insurers bargain with providers to get the lowest price possible. Traditional insurers were never able to negotiate very low rates with providers, because they had a commitment to letting patients see whichever doctors they wanted. Managed care insurers, in contrast, do not feel a need for universal access. People need a place to go to get bypass surgery, but do they have to be allowed to see every surgeon in town? In choosing which physicians to contract, low price is one criterion that insurers use.

Price reductions have saved insurers a lot of money. We do not have systematic evidence on how much managed care pays doctors relative to traditional fee-for-service insurance, but it is probably about 30 percent less.[2] Doctors accept these discounts because they have no choice. Some left the profession and others retired early when payments were cut, but most have put up with their lower incomes.[3]

Because not all managed care insurers use the same payment systems, the overall reimbursement system is a mess. Physicians might be paid an all-inclusive rate for some patients, a discounted fee-for-service basis for other patients, and a combination of the two for others. Most doctors have only a vague idea of how much they earn for each patient they treat.

In practice, doctors tend to consider the managed care era significantly less generous than the fee-for-service system, although not cataclysmically so. They are generally still paid more for doing more, but not nearly as much as previously.

On the patient side, managed care is in some ways more generous than the traditional system. In exchange for tighter restrictions on utilization of services, managed care charges much less for care used. Most managed care plans charge $5 or $10 per medical care visit, substantially less than what people would pay with traditional policies (provided they hadn't exceeded the maximum annual payment).[4] Thus, preventive care is encouraged. The goal of managed care is not to keep people out of the medical system entirely, just to limit what services they use when they enter it.

Managed care has had a profound effect on all aspects of the medical system, bringing about the first sustained reduction in medical care cost growth since 1950 (see table). From the early 1990s until very recently, medical care costs rose no more rapidly than GDP, ending a three-decade trend of cost increases. The reduction in costs from what was forecast as late as 1993 is about $400 per person per year—a very significant amount.

But what about the quality of medical care? Evaluating the effect of managed care on health is tricky. We can (sometimes) learn what services people receive in different plans, and how basic measures

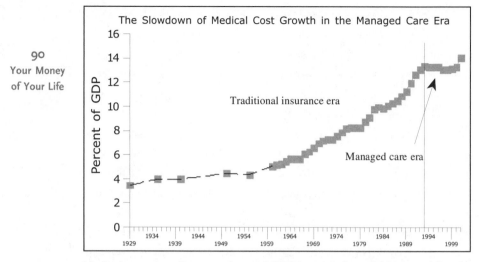

The Slowdown of Medical Cost Growth in the Managed Care Era

Medical care spending as a share of GDP increased particularly rapidly after 1960. Beginning in the early 1990s, spending was virtually constant as a share of GDP through 2000, before again starting to increase. (United States Department of Health and Human Services, Centers for Medicare and Medicaid Services, Office of the Actuary)

of health outcomes compare across plans. But these comparisons are complicated by the fact that people select which plan to join. Sicker people naturally prefer traditional insurance plans more than do healthier people. Without controlling for who chooses which plan, one would find that managed care improves health relative to traditional insurance, just because it enrolls healthier people. The good studies looking at the effects of managed care have attempted to control for how healthy people were before joining the plan, although there are varying degrees of success in doing this.[5]

It is clear that treatments for some conditions differ substantially under managed care plans. Depressed patients in managed care plans are more likely to be given medication than to receive psychotherapy, for example.[6] Of course, the evidence presented earlier in the book suggests that drugs may be more effective than psychotherapy for many people with depression, so this switch is not necessarily a bad one. For people with other conditions, there is more debate about the effect of managed care. Some studies have found that intensive surgery for heart disease is less common in managed care plans than in traditional insurance plans,[7] but that finding is by no means universal.[8] And offsetting the possible reduction in the use of very invasive care is some evidence of an increase in the use of less intensive services in managed care, such as aspirin on admission to the hospital and beta-blockers on discharge.[9] But the differences are relatively minor.

In keeping with the small overall effects of managed care on treatments provided, researchers who have looked directly at health outcomes under different insurance plans have not found a big difference between managed care and traditional insurance.[10] Survival rates after a heart attack are very similar for the two groups, and recovery from depression seems to be about the same. Overall, a few studies find worse outcomes in managed care plans, a few find better outcomes, and many find that health is no different.[11]

The cost savings from managed care have spilled over to the traditional insurance sector as well. Doctors who treat predominantly managed care patients practice in a different way, and this affects all of their patients. For example, hospitals acquire new technologies less frequently when managed care is more common[12] and use what is acquired less often.[13] On the other hand, use of preventive care is somewhat greater in areas with more managed care enrollment.[14] There is little evidence of adverse health outcomes for people living in areas with greater managed care enrollment.[15]

To date, therefore, managed care has lowered medical spending but not led to worse care. These spending reductions have been realized throughout the system.

In one sense, these findings are good news. Peoples' worst fears about managed care are overblown. In another sense, though, the news is not so good. Managed care was conceived as a way to improve health, not just save money. But there is no evidence that managed care has done much to improve quality of care.

By thinking about the incentives it creates, we can understand why managed care has had this effect. Recall the analysis in the previous chapter, differentiating care based on its technical sophistication and value. Traditional insurance reimbursed intensive services well, and less intensive care poorly. As a result, it encouraged all forms of intensive care, whether valuable or not, and discouraged use of less intensive care.

The incentives under managed care are somewhat different. By lowering payments to doctors and reviewing utilization, managed care discourages provision of the most intensive care. At the other end, reducing cost sharing for patients and having doctors share in the costs of complications encourage more use of routine and chronic disease care. In general, managed care is somewhat less friendly to more intensive care and friendlier to less intensive care. The system responded to these incentives in a predictable way. Somewhat less high-tech care is provided in managed care, but there is more routine and chronic disease care. Overall, there was not an enormous change, except that providers earn less and medical spending is lower.

This change has some good features, but it is not ideal. Routine care is still not encouraged sufficiently. Managed care gives physicians incentives to see patients in primary care settings—to prevent complications down the road—but does not allow enough time per visit. Doctors facing managed care treatment standards are unable to spend enough time with any one patient. Similarly, having office personnel follow up for people with chronic disease is more difficult when physician reimbursements are being cut. Thus, routine care does not increase.

For the more intensive procedures, managed care makes little distinction between more and less valuable care. Managed care has cut surgeons' fees but has not increased their incentives to operate on the neediest patients. Indeed, the incentives are perverse: surgeons facing lower reimbursement may cut back on the most difficult cases, even if these are the patients who benefit the most, if they are reimbursed equally for all. Managed care uses a meat ax to save money, when a scalpel is what is needed.

Over the longer term, the incentives under managed care could be quite damaging. Reducing use of high-tech care and paying less when the care is provided suggests that managed care could discourage new innovations. These types of innovations have been of enormous benefit to society, and it would be very bad for the system to discourage them.

So far, managed care does not seem to have affected medical research and development to any great extent. Pharmaceutical company spending on research and development increased in the 1990s at roughly the same rate as in prior decades. There are no comparable figures for the medical device industry, but the pace of technological innovation in that industry is rapid as well. Research and development has stayed high in part because managed care encourages the use of many pharmaceuticals. While the prices paid for medications are lower than they used to be, managed care often substitutes pharmaceuticals for more expensive surgeries or specialist care. This increases revenue for pharmaceutical companies.

On the noncommercial side, managed care has greatly reduced the ability of independent researchers to pursue their research. With payment reductions to hospitals and doctors, there is significantly less money for institutionally supported research than there once was. Fortunately, there has been a large increase in publicly supported biomedical research. The budget for the National Institutes of Health doubled between the late 1990s and 2002, cushioning the effect of lower patient-care revenue on research. On net, noncommercial research has held steady.

Of course, the situation for medical research and development may change in the future. The recent increase in the cost of prescription drugs has managed care companies turning their attention to that area. If cost cutting focuses on these products, the value of pharmaceutical innovation could fall. Noncommercial research will certainly suffer if National Institutes of Health funding declines.

The empirical evidence on the effect of managed care raises a fundamental question: If managed care saves money and does not compromise health, why do people hate it so much? The majority of health analysts, who have seen the studies described above, believe that managed care is a good thing. Spending is lower and outcomes are no worse. Encouraging managed care enrollment is still proposed as a model for Medicare reform, to help that program save money.

Managed care enrollees have a very different view. It is hard to overstate how much people hate managed care. Public opinion surveys show that managed care is among the most disliked of all industries, with roughly the support of tobacco and oil and gas companies. In *As Good As It Gets*, Helen Hunt earned raucous applause at one point, by unleasing a vulgar-filled tirade against managed care. How can analysts and the public think so differently?

One reason is simply that managed care has to do the dirty work of lowering spending. People clearly believe there is waste in the system; that fact has been demonstrated to almost everyone's satisfaction. But at the personal level, people got used to cheap, unlimited care. Managed care is the one telling people that they have to cut back, and so it takes the blame.

Managed care is also disliked because people do not believe that the money saved in managed care is getting back to them. If insurers pay doctors less and keep more themselves, how does that benefit average people? In fact, enrollees do save, but the chain is complex. The initial savings from cost reductions go to the managed care insurers. In the early 1990s, for example, as managed care was starting to cut payment rates, savings in the managed care industry were sizeable. Ultimately, though, businesses demanded the savings, in the form of lower premiums. They had pushed for managed care in the first place because they wanted to spend less on health insurance. Insurers had to comply to keep the business. So premiums fell. Indeed, they fell so much that many managed care plans nearly went bankrupt in the late 1990s. Their margins were small and costs unexpectedly rose.

But like a hot potato, the money kept moving. As employers made workers move into managed care, workers wanted to be compensated. An employer in a competitive market can't be that much less generous than his competitors, or employees would take jobs elsewhere. Thus, the money was ultimately paid to employees in the form of higher wages. Slow growth of health insurance costs is one reason that incomes grew so rapidly in the 1990s.

This path is so indirect that most people do not readily associate managed care with additional income. In a 1997 survey, 72 percent of people thought that money saved by managed care plans went to insurance company profits, and 56 percent thought that it allowed employers to pay less for medical care (people were allowed to give more than one answer).[16] Only 49 percent thought it made health care more affordable for people. Without perceiving themselves as getting much benefit, it is natural that people dislike managed care.

Fundamentally, though, people dislike managed care because they believe it lowers the quality and raises the inconvenience of medical care. People sense, and doctors tell people, that doctors are overworked by managed care. Office visits are shorter; waiting times are longer; and referrals are harder to make. Stories about poorer health outcomes in managed care are legendary. A few examples:

A child with cancer is denied the treatment necessary to save his life.

A woman loses her baby in the last trimester of her pregnancy, because her HMO overruled her doctor's recommendation and refused to cover a hospital stay to monitor her high-risk case.

A woman dies because she falls ill on vacation, and her insurance company insists that she fly home to be treated by doctors in the plan, even though a physician warned in advance that the flight could kill her.

A 36-year-old father dies after an HMO repeatedly denies access to his regular cardiologist, despite promises from the HMO of continued access to that specialist when he enrolled in that HMO. After months of delay, the plan finally authorized an appointment with the cardiologist, but the patient died the day before the scheduled visit.

A San Diego paraplegic asks for referral to a rehabilitation specialist. Her HMO refuses, and she develops a severe pressure wound that the specialist would have routinely checked and treated. She is forced to undergo surgery, and is hospitalized for a year with round-the-clock nursing care.

A woman with breast cancer is sent home hours after a mastectomy—against doctor's orders—in pain and with drainage tubes still in place. Later, she is denied coverage for reconstructive surgery, because the insurance company says the surgery is cosmetic.[17]

As we have seen, these failures are not widespread. There is no evidence of systematically worse health outcomes as a whole. But the stories jibe with what people believe is the ethos of the system. People sense that the goal of health insurance has shifted away from improving their health to increasing profit. People like to save money, but not at the expense of their health.

If insurance companies wanted, they could emphasize quality improvement as much as cost reduction. They could invest in computer and information systems so that patients could use the system more easily. They could encourage better care management for people with chronic disease. These are not impossible goals. Some insurers take these steps, but the industry has not done so to nearly the extent it could.

This lack of responsiveness is particularly surprising economically. Insurance is a competitive industry. Normally, we think that competition gives people what they want. If people want high quality and low cost, the market should give it to them. If existing insurers won't, new ones will. But the market has not responded to peoples' desire to be healthier. Why not? The fundamental reason is that it is not profitable for insurers to provide quality. Insurers that attempt to improve the quality of care their enrollees receive will wind up losing money, not making it. Thus, quality-improvement initiatives are rarely adopted.

There are several reasons that quality is not profitable. One reason is free riding: Any individual insurer that invests in quality improvement cannot keep the benefits of those programs to itself.[18] Consider an insurer that helps the doctors with whom it contracts improve quality. It might pay for computer systems, extra nurses, patient reminders, education efforts, and so on. Most doctors have contracts with many insurance companies. As a result, when doctors put the new systems in place, they are likely to treat all their patients that way. But this means that the insurer paying for the quality effort gets few benefits from it. People don't have to enroll in its plan to get the new services. Nor will current enrollees pay more for that plan; they can always switch to another plan and keep their doctor. The incentives for quality improvement are thus blunted.

Some evidence of the importance of the free-rider problem can be found by examining the health plans that have taken the biggest quality-improvement initiatives. The success stories—HealthPartners in Minneapolis, Group Health Cooperative in Puget Sound, Kaiser Permanente in California, Independent Health in Buffalo, and others like them—generally (although not always) employ their own doctors full-time. Thus, if their doctors improve their care management, all the benefits go to that health plan.

Beyond the free-rider problem, insurers find it difficult to charge more for higher quality. Many quality-improvement efforts cost money, at least in the short run, with savings coming only down the road. Since people change health plans frequently, however, an insurer that implements a quality-improvement program has to pay all the up-front costs but frequently will not realize the savings.

In principle, insurers could make up for this by charging higher premiums to businesses when they implement the program. Businesses could handle the higher up-front costs by granting less rapid pay increases, or by realizing longer-term savings. In practice, though, insurers have great difficulty charging businesses for this type of investment. Insurers uniformly complain that they are unable to raise premiums and maintain market share, even if the money goes for quality-improvement programs. Businesses are unwilling to absorb the short-term costs of higher quality.

A final barrier to quality improvement is that high quality might attract more patients, but these may be the wrong kind of patients. Suppose that one health plan in a market develops a reputation for very high-quality diabetes care. Diabetics living in the area would soon learn about the program and switch to it. More enrollees means greater premium revenues, but diabetic enrollees cost a lot to treat, even if they are well managed. Plans could thus lose money by attracting more diabetics, even if their care is truly first rate.

This phenomenon of high quality being unprofitable is termed adverse selection.[19] Adverse selection differentiates medical care from most other industries. In the automobile industry, every car off the same assembly line costs the same amount to build and sells for roughly the same price. Thus, having a reputation for building high-quality cars brings in more customers and the same profits from each customer. In health insurance, the cost of supplying the good depends on who buys it. If sick people especially prefer quality care, plans will lose money by offering higher quality.

In response to these selection concerns plans prefer to prevent high-risk people from enrolling. That is usually not feasible—most employers do not allow this. But there are alternatives. Plans can solicit enrollees in wealthy neighborhoods, where people are on average healthier, and avoid downtrodden areas where the population is on average less healthy. They can spend large resources on well-baby care (to attract healthy women) but cut back on care for the mentally ill. They can raise the cost sharing on syringes and insulin to make it more difficult for diabetics to be in the plan. (In Germany, one plan wrote a letter to its diabetic members pointing out that another plan was far superior on diabetes care; the plan that was noted to be better complained). All these measures affect plan enrollment and are difficult for government to police.

For all these reasons, quality improvement is not a major focus of health insurance. Cost reduction is, and it permeates the system. Every health insurer in the country is constantly considering ways to cut costs. This focus is noticeable, and it makes people upset, justifiably.

Firms do not survive if they do not produce goods that people want. Managed care is not a good that people really want. It will not survive in its current form. The beginning of the end is already at hand. In recent years, managed care plans have removed some of their most onerous restrictions. For example, United Health Care, one of the largest HMOs in the country, decided in 1999 to end preauthorization requirements for most major procedures. The outrage caused by the requirement was just too great. Managed care is easing up in area after area, in response to consumer and physician complaints (not surprisingly, the easing up has been accompanied by an increase in medical care costs evident in the table earlier in the chapter). The strict managed care era is already on the way out.

Managed care has taught us a fundamental lesson about what we want out of medicine. We are interested not just in cost savings but in health improvement. In the next two chapters, I explain how we can get health improvement and make it affordable.

9

PAYING FOR HEALTH

THERE ARE TWO MAJOR CHALLENGES in medical care: finding a means to insure the uninsured and designing a system that improves the value of what we get. In this and the next chapter, I present ways to address these issues. I start here with suggestions about improving the quality of care for the insured; and then turn to the issue of the uninsured.

To understand quality improvement, start with a simple observation: You get what you pay for. Anyone who has ever remodeled their house knows this, and it applies to the medical system as well. We want the medical system to improve our health, but we reimburse it for treating us when we're sick. Medical care is not the same as health improvement, and the system does poorly when they differ. A better medical care system would pay for health improvement, rather than for provision of services.

To see how such a system would work, consider the current Medicare program. When a doctor sees Medicare patients now, he or she submits a bill to the government for each visit, describing the diagnosis and treatment. Payment is based purely on the services provided.

Now suppose that the government added an additional payment at the end of the year linked to the overall quality of care that the doctor had provided. For example, if the doctor had ordered cholesterol screenings for people at high risk for cardiovascular disease, he would receive a bonus. Ordering mammograms for women at risk for cancer, or administering flu shots to the elderly would also qualify for a bonus. The total bonus might be as much as 10 percent of total income. Hospitals would qualify for bonuses, too, based on their own quality criteria. Hospitals with lower mortality rates for bypass surgery or fewer surgical complications would receive bonuses.

Providers would think differently under such a system. If there were additional income to be earned by making sure cholesterol tests were performed, doctors would figure out how to increase testing. Physician offices would set up reminder systems. Nurses would contact patients to arrange convenient times. Outreach would be facilitated. Hospitals would similarly search for ways to improve bypass surgery mortality and cut postoperative infection. The money that would follow would make it possible for providers to spend time and resources focusing on this issue.

Such bonus payments could be made to insurers as well. Insurers that had more patients who got recommended screening, better risk-factor control, and good surgical outcomes would earn bonuses over those that did not. These financial incentives would give insurers an incentive to focus on quality improvement. They would work to steer patients to higher-volume, and thus higher-quality, hospitals, for example, and would better reimburse doctors with good track records.

The key to the quality-based payment system is that it differentiates between the intensity of medical care and the value of it, the distinction presented in the previous chapters. Current payment systems work only the basis of the intensity of services provided. Some reimburse high-intensity services well, and others reimburse it poorly, but intensity is always the central feature. Health-based payments, in contrast, reward high-value services regardless of their intensity. Thus, there are no incentives to overprovide or underprovide services.

Compared to other reimbursement systems, quality-based payments also rationalize the incentives for new technologies. In the fee-for-service insurance era, the development of intensive technologies was encouraged, while the development of less intensive technologies was not. In the managed care era, intensive technologies are discouraged because of their high cost. If health improvement were rewarded, doctors would be eager to adopt innovations that had a high value, whether they were intensive or not. The changed incentives for technology utilization would in turn feed technology development.

Implementing health-based payments in practice will require coordinated public- and private-sector actions. Government and private insurers each pay for about 40 percent of medical care (the rest is paid directly by families). To be maximally effective in influencing provider incentives, the public and private sectors would need to use similar payment systems. A physician paid for diabetes control one way by the government and another way by the private sector might simply throw up his hands and ignore them both.

The public and private sectors can coordinate in two ways. One strategy is for the government to take the lead in developing quality guidelines and to promulgate them throughout the medical system. Some insurers may accept such guidelines willingly. In other cases, government can induce private insurers to adopt them by paying insurers based on compliance. If the quality system adopted by the government highlights cholesterol screening, mammography, and flu shots, for example, the government could require insurers to report their performance on these dimensions and could make supplemental payments to insurers based on how well they do. Paying insurers bonuses based on quality performance would induce insurers to use those quality standards to determine payments to physicians.

Government action is often slow, however. Public authorities have difficulty enacting policies that have not received support in the private sector. The second strategy, therefore, is for private businesses to develop such a system and encourage government to go along. The private sector has recently started efforts along these lines. The most important development is the creation of the "Leapfrog Group," an organization of many of the largest firms in America, which is focused on reducing medical errors in hospitals. The Leapfrog Group keeps track of medical errors and the safety innovations—for example, a computerized system for entering physician orders—that different hospitals make. The quality data are published for consumers, and some employers are starting to use it to calculate payments—paying more to hospitals that adopt these safety innovations. If this effort expands, it could form the basis of a national system.

It all sounds simple—pay more for effective care. But how do we know it will work? Economists are famous for the extent to which they dream unworkable ideas. We joke about it ourselves. Q: How does an economist stranded on a desert island open a can of peas? A: He assumes he has a can opener. Before embarking on such a program, we need some sense that it will be effective. Let me present the reasons that I am optimistic, and then discuss the complications.

The history of medical care in the United States, which is described throughout this book, suggests that providing the right incentives will generate the responses we want. Recall how money changed the diagnosis and treatment of depression. Prior to the Prozac era, half of all patients with depression were not appropriately diagnosed, and many of those diagnosed were not prescribed appropriate therapy. Pleading with the system to do better did not help; there were any number of consensus statements and calls to action. But financial incentives worked. When the pharmaceutical companies developed effective treatments for depression, they had an incentive to increase diagnosis. The companies informed doctors and patients about depression and how it could be treated. Within a decade, diagnoses of depression doubled. To be sure, there was overuse associated with this incentive, but the incentives were not structured to encourage appropriate use—only to increase total use.

There are a few important cases in which quality of medical care has been publicly reported, and reporting seems to have improved outcomes. I recently saw an example of how such a system can work. I looked at the control of diabetes at HealthPartners, a large insurer (an HMO, no less) in Minneapolis, Minnesota.[1] Several years ago, HealthPartners decided to reconfigure its patient practice to improve the quality of the diabetes care it provided to its members. Four times a year, HealthPartners compiles a list of each physician's diabetic patients and distributes the list to its physicians. The list details when each patient last had key tests performed and gives relevant clinical results of those tests. It also provides information about when new tests should be scheduled. While doctors had this information in their records, most had never looked at it in a systematic way.

Doctors have responded to knowing more about their patients. When a patient neglects to have a test by the recommended time, a nurse calls the patient to urge him or her to come in. Through guidelines and regular feedback, physicians and nurses are taught to manage the disease better. Diabetes education nurses are available to give consultations and make referrals to specialists. In addition to providing information, HealthPartners pays a bonus to physician groups that manage diabetes well. The bonus is not large, but it helps offset the costs of the practice changes.

The system works. There has been a marked decrease in the share of diabetics with uncontrolled blood-sugar levels since the program started. More diabetics are on medication, and more get regular tests. Increased service use raised costs in the short term, of course. But the health improvements far outweigh the cost of the program.[2]

Implementing this type of program is not rocket science. There is nothing unique about HealthPartners or the steps it took that make its results impossible to duplicate. Indeed, similar examples exist at Independent Health Association, an HMO in Buffalo, and Group Health Cooperative in Seattle, among other places. Improving medical care quality is possible, if that is the goal of the system.

The longest-standing effort at quality measurement is in New York State. In the late 1980s, New York state officials wanted to evaluate the quality of bypass surgery and angioplasty operations performed in the state. To measure quality, the state gathered data on mortality for people receiving these procedures. They adjusted mortality for the sickness of the patient, so that doctors with more impaired patients were not seen as providing poorer quality care. The results revealed a large variation in quality. The best hospitals have mortality rates that are one-fifth those of the worst hospitals.[3] The spread among individual physicians is even greater.

Just publishing the quality information has had a salutary effect.

Since the data were published, many hospitals with low rankings have undertaken quality-improvement programs.[4] Some hospitals prohibit surgery by surgeons who operate infrequently, recognizing the link between volume and outcomes. In other cases, hospitals recruited new cardiac surgery chiefs and made changes in the surgical process. In still other cases, surgeons were encouraged to specialize in particular types of patients, since they seemed to do well with certain groups. The net result was a large decline in cardiac surgery mortality in New York State. We do not know if this decline would have occurred without the reporting system, but most analysts suspect reporting helped.[5] As a result of its perceived success, the New York state system has been copied by California, Massachusetts, New Jersey, and Pennsylvania.

A major effort has also been made to measure the quality of different insurance plans. An organization called the National Committee for Quality Assurance, or NCQA for short, has pioneered this effort. NCQA was originally formed by managed care insurers to fend off federal quality monitoring. For much of its early life, its goal was to deter inquires into true quality. In the early 1990s, though, NCQA had a change of heart and decided to measure the quality of medical care for real.

The NCQA quality measure is termed the Health Plan Employer Data and Information Set (HEDIS). Its measures include process features, such as whether patients receive beta-blockers after a heart attack; measures of patient satisfaction with care received; and data on risk-factor control. Insurers care a great deal about their HEDIS ranking, advertising the results if positive and undertaking steps to improve scores if negative. Indeed, the publication of the HEDIS data has been associated with higher plan quality. For example, the use of beta-blockers after a heart attack rose from about 60 percent in 1996, the first year it was measured, to more than 90 percent by 2000. In addition, quality improved for diabetes treatment, breast cancer screening, and cholesterol screening.[6]

Employers have also been involved in pushing for quality improvement. In addition to the Leapfrog Group, business coalitions in California[7] and Minneapolis[8] have pushed providers to focus on improving quality, believing that reducing errors will not only improve health but also save money. Many of these business initiatives are new, and so no evaluation is possible. But the evidence from programs that have been in place for a while suggests that they improve the situation. When businesses focus on quality improvement, providers and insurers do the same. None of the programs has led to a major transformation of the medical system, but one would not expect relatively small programs to have wide-reaching effects. The findings are encouraging, if not overwhelming.

Other evidence on the likely efficacy of health-based payments comes from outside the medical system, in the area of environmental advocacy. As is well known, some economic activities are inherently unfriendly to the environment. Electricity production requires air pollution, for example, which leads to problems such as global warming and acid rain. The control of acid rain illustrates the great success that economic incentives can have.

The history of economic incentives in acid rain control goes back three decades. The Clean Air Act of 1970 established standards for the maximum amount of sulfur dioxide in the air (the leading cause of acid rain).[9] The act did not use economic incentives. Instead it regulated pollution output at particular plants and even mandated specific forms of pollution abatement by firms. Generally, these regulations applied to newer power plants, since retrofitting older plants would be very costly. It was assumed that over time, old plants would close, and new plants would already be complying.

But this did not happen. Because older power plants were not regulated very tightly and were thus cheaper to run, firms kept them running even after they should have been replaced. Further, there was little incentive for firms to make technological innovations in new plants other than the mandatory ones, since there was no economic reward for doing so. Overall, acid rain control was not great, and the regulatory burden was high.

Economists proposed a different solution. Rather than regulating the steps that had to be taken to limit pollution, they argued for limiting sulfur dioxide emissions in total, since that is what we ultimately care about. Electricity producers could then control sulfur dioxide in any way they saw fit. This is similar to arguing that we should pay for the ultimate outcome we care about (health), and let providers decide on the intermediate steps (medical treatments).

After many years of fruitless arguing, the economic solution was finally tried. A sulfur dioxide permit system was created in the early 1990s. Firms were issued permits that allowed them a certain amount of sulfur dioxide output. They could buy and sell the permits and even store them for future use, but they could not pollute more than allowed by the permits they had.

The results have been excellent.[10] In the first few years of operation, there was actually less pollution than the permits allowed, as firms stored pollution rights for future use. Further, the costs of meeting the emissions targets have been much smaller than they were under the old system, as firms have found cheaper ways of limiting pollution than the older act had specified. The tradeable permit system is widely seen as a great success and a model for future environmental regulation. The lesson for health is that focusing on the right goal and providing incentives to meet that goal can make an enormous difference.

There are two potential problems that need to be overcome to make a quality-based payment system work. If these problems can be surmounted—and I believe they can—a quality-based payment system would likely be successful. Others analysts are more skeptical. Let me illustrate the problems and possible solutions.

The first issue is how to measure quality. Quality is multidimensional; how are we to determine if a doctor provides high- or low-quality care? Adding to the difficulty of making this assessment is that some measures of quality are beyond the provider's control; punishing the doctor for things he or she can do nothing about would not be good. In practice, the measures of quality have to be carefully designed and tailored to the specific setting—one for individual physicians, a second for hospitals and other institutions, and a third for insurance companies.

There are several dimensions of quality that *can* be measured. The care process is one. Are diabetics having their blood sugar tested at recommended intervals? Are children vaccinated on schedule? Are women receiving mammograms? Recommendations about appropriate care are relatively common; groups such as the U.S. Preventive Services Task Force and physician specialty organizations provide them. These guidelines would be particularly appropriate in evaluating physicians.

Health outcomes are also measurable. Risk-factor control is a crucial part of maintaining health. Diabetics should have their blood sugar at acceptable levels, people with high cholesterol should have controlled cholesterol, and hypertensives should meet blood pressure guidelines. We can also measure physical outcomes such as cardiovascular disease mortality and cancer mortality. Nonfatal outcomes include physical functioning after a stroke (for example, how much the person can walk) or mental health after depression (using common depression questionnaires). Outcome measures are better for rating health plans and large hospitals than for rating particular physicians. For any given doctor, there is too much uncertainty in the outcomes of his patients for the measure of outcomes to be of much use.

Patient satisfaction would also be part of a quality system. Being able to see doctors at convenient times, to communicate with providers easily, and to work through the system are important dimensions of quality. Survey instruments to measure patient satisfaction have already been developed and could be used to gauge this measure of quality.[11]

The exact determination of what is to be measured for the many different medical care providers will require additional analysis. So will the specific bonus amount for each item.[12] The important point is that it can be done.

In creating these measures, we need to ensure that health plans do not manipulate the data they use to measure quality. If insurers are paid for controlling blood pressure in hypertensives, for example, they cannot be allowed to call everyone a hypertensive, knowing that most will be "controlled" when blood pressure is actually tested. The meltdown in accounting standards we recently witnessed—the demise of Enron, Arthur Anderson, and others—highlights the importance of monitoring information gathering. Data-collection procedures have to be laid out in detail. Independent auditors must verify what plans report. Penalties for cheating must be severe, including jail time and removal from the system. An independent body, separate from the industry, must monitor the whole process. One hopes that we have learned enough to set up a system that works.

The second difficult issue with a health-based payment system is the potential adverse incentives it creates for providers to serve only those who are easy to manage. If insurers make money by successfully treating people with high cholesterol, they will seek to insure people who are better able to follow medication instructions. If hospitals are paid for good surgical outcomes, they will want to operate on only the healthiest people. These responses harm the system. It is the people who do not take good care of themselves or who are more difficult surgical candidates whom it is important to treat.

This situation is familiar; it is adverse selection all over again. In the current market, health plans make money by insuring the people who cost the least to serve. Health plans avoid quality-improvement efforts for fear they will attract the less healthy. In this alternate system, plans would discourage people who are sick in ways that are hard to control from enrolling. If it is more difficult for poor people to manage their cholesterol than it is for rich people—for example, dietary change is harder, or medication management is more difficult to sustain—health plans will want to insure the rich but not the poor.

There is a way to manage the adverse selection problem. The key is to give more credit to outcome improvements among harder-to-manage groups. For example, a plan that manages to reduce high cholesterol rates among the poor by 10 percent might get just as much credit for bonus calculations as a plan that engenders a 20 percent reduction among the rich. If the relative benchmarks are set correctly, insurers will not want to take the rich over the poor. Indeed, the poor could even be prized enrollees if the targets for them are easier to meet.

Medical researchers term such a system "risk adjustment"—it adjusts observed outcomes for the difference in patient backgrounds.

Risk adjustment can incorporate medical as well as social factors; anything that influences how hard it is to meet bonus goals could be part of the risk- adjustment system.

Health care researchers are hard at work designing risk-adjustment systems. Doing simple risk adjustment is easy; we can readily measure who is very sick and who is not. But more complete risk adjustment is harder. For which groups is it really possible to design effective interventions? The work to date has focused on designing systems to ensure that insurance plans in the current system do not have incentives to discourage the sick from enrolling. The problem of risk adjustment for a health-based payment system is similar.

Experts' views about health-based payments are directly related to whether they think quality can be accurately measured, and whether risk adjustment is likely to succeed. I believe these problems can be surmounted and am thus optimistic. Others believe that these problems are too tough for us to handle.

The approach to medical care quality improvement that I have outlined is very different from the approaches that most others advocate. The political system's most common response to quality concerns is to propose new regulations. Hospitals could be required to invest in safety systems, doctors could have to certify that they know about certain types of therapies, insurance companies could be required to cover certain services, and so on. Regulation is appealing because of the certainty it affords.

But regulation is extraordinarily difficult in an industry as complex as medical care. Should a large city hospital and a small rural hospital both have the same computerized prescription order system? Who is to say that one type of system is right for everybody? Further, regulation is inherently adversarial. Providers want to practice medicine their own way, but they are constrained by regulation from doing so. Exceptions are complex and time-consuming. Everyone gets upset.

The United States has tried regulating medical care before, and it failed.[13] In the 1970s many states had so-called Certificate of Need programs that required hospitals to get governmental approval before investing in new technologies. The idea was that new technologies were contributing to medical care cost growth, and that such technologies were overused—both legitimate premises. Requiring applications before such technologies could be acquired seemed logical.

In practice, governments were never really able to determine when new technologies were needed and when they were not. Costs and benefits are rarely known in advance. Further, the political influence of hospitals and communities guaranteed that most proposals were approved. Ultimately, cost growth was unaffected. If we couldn't regulate 5,000 hospitals' purchases of a few simple acquisitions, what basis do we have for thinking we can regulate millions of medical interactions each year?

Another common response to poor quality is to make it easier for people to sue their insurers and providers. If patients were able to sue insurers more readily for substandard care, insurers might pay more attention to the care provided. The same is true for doctors. There is certainly some deterrent value to litigation, and people should be compensated when something bad happens to a loved one. But more litigation is not the answer here. Litigation encourages hiding mistakes, when what we need is for providers to admit them and learn from them. The threat of litigation creates a silo mentality, with insurers against doctors, and doctors against each other. Mistakes are corrected through cooperation, not conflict. The recent strikes by doctors in New Jersey and West Virginia in January and February 2003, show how adversarial medical malpractice lawsuits are. Good doctors are driven to outrage, or even out of business, by malpractice concerns, while bad doctors are not sufficiently punished.

Regulation and litigation are flawed because they both work on the principle of punishment. The goal in each case is to restrict what doctors can do, or require them to do certain things. But punishment is not right here. Medical care is too complex for regulation to work effectively. For the system to work well, we need to create incentives for the system to work right. All the evidence we have suggests that this strategy will work.

That is not to say that everyone will support this idea. The most skeptical groups are likely to be medical care providers. Grading physicians on the quality of their practice will be upsetting to many, as it infringes on their clinical freedom.

Some opposition along these lines is unavoidable. Like everyone else, physicians prefer more autonomy in what they do. As we have seen, however, granting physicians complete autonomy—the old fee-for-service model—did not produce sufficiently good outcomes. The real choice for physicians is not between facing constraints and not. Rather, it is which constraint: regulation, increased malpractice scrutiny, or quality assessment and payment. In such a comparison, quality assessment is the far superior option.

Proponents of single-payer medical care systems, like the Canadian model and the current Medicare system, are also likely to oppose this system. A major concern of single-payer adherents is reducing administrative expenses in medicine and transferring the money saved into increased patient care. In contrast to the single-payer plans, plans that require measuring quality inherently involve increased administrative expenses. I am not particularly concerned by this, however. Fundamentally, the goal is to get medical care to the right people. If that involves an increased administrative burden, that is an appropriate cost.

Finally, some people who are more conservative will not support this idea because it focuses on provider payment and not individual costs as the key to reform. Many on the Right stress on patient payments rather than insurer payments. In this strategy, the key to health reform is to make people pay more for the medical care they receive. The idea is that consumers who are well informed and have a financial stake in their medical care decisions will choose valuable services and avoid less valuable ones.

Developing a well-informed consumer population is beneficial. But the idea that consumers armed with that information can navigate the system well on their own is not one that I share. We have seen many instances in which even very well insured patients do not receive services that are valuable. The vast majority of elderly people are insured for laboratory tests, for example, yet rates of mammography screening and cholesterol testing are still low. If the system does not work well for those with a strong financial incentive to access care, it will work even less well when people are made to pay more.

Ultimately, it is only a transformation of the medical care system that will change how it operates. The changes proposed here have the greatest chances of success.

10

UNIVERSAL BENEFITS

THE RATIONALE FOR UNIVERSAL IN-
surance coverage is clear. Just about everyone agrees that all people
should have health insurance. The question is how to make this happen. Increased insurance coverage necessarily requires government
action. The experience of the past decade teaches us that even a
booming economy will not lead to increased insurance coverage
without major public support. As a result, I focus on what government can do to increase insurance coverage.

There are two requirements for a system in which every family
has health insurance: There must be a place at which insurance can
be obtained, and there has to be a system of financing that makes
insurance affordable. Currently, it is not easy for families without
access to employer-based insurance to buy insurance. Those who are
not covered through an employer are left to deal with insurers on
their own. They may be denied coverage or offered insurance only
at high rates. Few wind up buying.

To address this, I would allow all families to purchase insurance
the way that government employees do.[1] The Federal government
currently provides health insurance to nine million workers, ranging
from the president and members of Congress to postal workers and
park rangers. The government organizes the system but is not the
insurer. Private insurers that want to cover federal workers submit
rates to the government and (if they qualify) their plans are then
offered to employees. To qualify, insurers must agree to cover all

people who want to enroll and to charge everyone the same premium. Thus, there are no denials based on ill health.

There is no reason that this system could not be expanded. Access to the insurance pool could be opened to anyone who wanted to join. People would not have to join—coverage could remain through an employer or other entity—but everyone would have the option.

The insurers in the federal pool have varying rates, depending on the benefits each plan offers. Traditional fee-for-service plans are more expensive than managed care plans. Some of this variability is good, reflecting the generosity of benefits that insurers provide. But part of the reason that more generous plans cost more than less generous plans is that more generous plans attract sicker people, who naturally cost more to treat. This is the adverse selection problem we witnessed previously. The federal government could, but does not, adjust premiums on the basis of enrollees' health status—the risk-adjustment method presented earlier. Doing so would make the system better.

In addition, the federal government does not pay plans on the basis of quality delivered. As we have seen, incentives in the current system are not strong enough to encourage the highest-quality care. As part of efforts to improve quality, the government should implement quality-based bonus payments.

The average premium for government policies mirrors that in the nation as a whole, about $3,000 for an individual and $8,000 for a family. Clearly, not everyone can afford these rates; a subsidy system is needed so that everyone can afford insurance. Offering subsidies to the poor sounds like a major undertaking, but in practice we already subsidize care for the poor. Eight thousand dollars a year is far too much for a lower-income family to afford; only one-third of families earning less than $25,000 per year have private health insurance.[2] Many low-income families are insured through Medicaid. Medicaid is financed through general taxation, the bulk of which is paid for by middle- and higher-income people. Another large share of the poor is uninsured. The services used by the uninsured are generally provided without charge to them. No services can be truly unreimbursed, however; hospitals must get some money to cover their costs. In practice, hospitals offset the costs of uncompensated care by charging more to public and private insurers, these changes are in turn passed along to middle- and upper-income people in the form of higher premiums and taxes.

A formal insurance system for the poor would involve some additional spending on medical care, but many of the costs are already being paid. The difference is that many of the current payments are not made by the government; they are made directly by the insured poor or indirectly by middle- and upper-income people, through higher health insurance premiums. Moving to a formal insurance system would bring these costs into the open and onto the public budget.

The design of a subsidy system to support universal coverage is a subject of much technical debate.[3] Most such subsidies are designed as tax credits—people get a lower tax bill, or a refund from the government, to be used to purchase insurance. The tax credit would be highest for poor people and would decline with increasing income. For example, the credit might be worth $7,000 for families below the poverty line, about $15,000 per year, and would phase out as incomes rose. The exact set of credits would depend on the revenues available. Needless to say, this last point is crucial; I will return to it later.

Even with generous credits, not everyone will choose to buy coverage. To guarantee universal coverage, we need to compel people to buy insurance.[4] This is a major step. In a voluntary insurance system like the current one, people have incentives to make the appropriate payments, or else they will not be covered. In a universal system, by contrast, people are guaranteed insurance, whether or not their check arrives on time. Thus, the onus is on the government to force people to pay—having a government agency checking to ensure that payments are made, chasing people down when they are not, and fining habitual offenders. Universal coverage necessarily means a larger role for government than is the case now.

The biggest difficulty in this or any universal coverage proposal is financing. Where does the government get the money to offset the cost of the tax credits? Put another way, the tax credits that the government can afford clearly depend on the available revenue. The foregone revenue from a comprehensive tax credit system is significant; a system like that proposed here might amount to about 5 percent of total federal spending.[5] In 1993 the Clinton administration's solution to the financing problem was to reduce the growth rates of allowed payments to hospitals and physicians under Medicare and Medicaid and use the savings to pay for expanded coverage. Although the Clinton plan was not enacted, Medicare and Medicaid costs increased far less rapidly in the 1990s than had previously been forecast. Along with the booming economy, savings in those programs were a major reason that the federal budget was in surplus in the late 1990s.

Boom times do not last forever, and the boom of the 1990s was followed by a prolonged recession. Government budgets always get worse when the economy fares poorly. Like the phases of the moon, though, what shrinks in one era rises in another. Recessions end, and a return to a good economy would have produced surpluses comparable to those we witnessed at the end of the 1990s. The money for major health insurance credits was thus at hand, if temporarily out of the bank account.

The Bush administration did not use the financial savings for expanded insurance coverage, however. Rather, it passed large tax cuts in 2001 and again in 2003 predominantly directed toward the wealthiest Americans. Of the total tax reduction, about one-third went to people in the top 1 percent of the income distribution. More than two-thirds went to people in the top 20 percent of the distribution.[6] That was a mistake; the benefits of health care program savings and the booming economy should have been used to finance benefits for all, not just the privileged few. To offset the credits that are required for universal insurance coverage, I would redirect the money in the Bush tax cuts to expanded health insurance.[7] Taxation would not increase; rather, existing tax savings would be redirected to everyone.

This money would be sufficient to cover health insurance credits for the next several years, but would not be sufficient beyond that. If medical costs continue to increase more rapidly than tax revenues, as they have in the past, the same level of federal revenues will not be able to support an increasingly expensive medical care program, even in good economic times. This is true whether one looks at the current situation or a plan for universal coverage; Medicare and Medicaid are not sustainable given their historical growth rates and federal revenues forecasts.

The only solution is to devote more resources to government medical care programs over time. We saw the scale of government expand dramatically when Social Security was created. We will need to expand it again to meet the medical care burden. The only other alternatives—restricting the growth of medical costs or crowding out other items in the public budget—are not real options.

There are two other common proposals for universal insurance coverage beyond the strategy outlined here. They would both cover everyone, but I believe they are inferior for other reasons. The first alternative is the single-payer system.[8] Under this approach, the government would levy a new income tax, the proceeds from which would be used to pay for medical care for the population as a whole. Existing private insurance coverage would be eliminated. As with Medicare and the Canadian medical care system, the government would determine what services would be covered, how much doctors would be paid, and what utilization review methods would be used.

Most single-payer systems have a number of features beyond the provision of public insurance. The limits on the availability of high-tech treatments in Canada were discussed earlier. Technological restrictions are not intrinsic to single-payer systems, however. Single-payer systems could be less constrained, as Medicare is now. Alternatively, private insurance systems could be constrained, as they are in Germany and in managed care plans in the United States. The important issue in this discussion is that single-payer systems involve only one insurer, not that use is tightly restricted.

Choosing between a government-run insurance system and a private system is a major decision. In most markets, we believe that competition is good—and by implication that private provision is superior to government provision. Firms that compete seek to raise quality and lower costs, both of which are valuable. As we have seen, however, competition in health insurance does not necessarily lead to better outcomes. The possibility of adverse selection makes insurers leery of offering any benefit that appeals to less healthy people. The difficulty of appropriating benefits also generates weak incentives for quality improvement. On top of this, private insurance involves higher administrative costs than does public insurance.[9] Many people look at this list of drawbacks and opt for a public system.

These problems can be addressed, however, at least in principle. Bonus payments can be made to health insurers for quality improvements that promote health. Payments to health plans can also be adjusted for the health risk of enrollees, to reduce adverse selection. If we make these reforms, a private system could generate better outcomes. I am optimistic about our ability to design better systems, and thus I am not in favor of a single-payer insurance system. If this optimism turned out to be misplaced, however, the single-payer system would look increasingly attractive.

The second alternative is to require employers to pay for health insurance.[10] Many employers now offer health insurance; those that do not would be required to start. Employers would have to pay for about 80 percent of the premium; employees would pay the remainder. Nonworkers would be responsible for the entire amount on their own, but low-income families would receive subsidies. Subsidies would also go to small firms, or firms with many low-wage employees.

The Clinton plan took this approach to universal coverage. All employers were required to pay for part of insurance, with families paying the rest. The employer mandate was a key part of the Clinton plan's financing.

Public discussion of mandating payments for employers is frequently off point. When people are asked whether they want to pay for insurance themselves or have their employer pay, most people choose the latter. Who wouldn't? However, although firms write the check for health insurance, they do not actually bear the burden of the payments. The real costs are borne by workers.

The reason is straightforward. When employers pay more to health insurers, there are only a few ways that employers can respond: They can charge higher prices for their goods; they can pay less to workers; or they can realize lower profits. Raising prices is not really possible; markets are too competitive for that. Similarly, profits cannot fall by much, or people would be unwilling to invest in firms. The only real solution is to reduce the rate of wage increases. Indeed, if wage growth did not slow, employers would be forced to fire workers.

From workers' perspectives, giving up wage increases is not so bad, because at least the workers get health insurance. So workers accept the wage trade-off. Economically, having employers pay is simply a roundabout way of charging workers for insurance.

The implication of this offset is that workers would bear the burden of an employer-based payment system just as much as they bear the burden of mandated individual payments. There is no difference between these proposals in who really pays for insurance. The major difference between them is which system is easiest to administer. The individual approach is clearly superior in this dimension. In the employer approach, there are enormous difficulties associated with determining how people get covered. If a family has two workers, which employer pays for coverage? If one person loses a job, how fast must payments from the other employer increase? Must workers tell their boss when a spouse becomes unemployed or they get divorced? Similarly, there are difficulties with job mobility. With employer-based insurance, changing jobs often means changing doctors and access to particular medications. This does not happen when individuals pay.

Health insurance is not something that is made better by tying it to employment. As a result, essentially all economists believe that universal coverage should be done outside of employment.

———————

The solution proposed here combines elements of proposals favored by the political Left and Right. Those on the political Left are strong proponents of progressive financing of health benefits. The tax credits proposed here provide this progressivity. Those on the Right generally dislike government intervention in markets. This plan limits government involvement to organizing an effective market and providing money to make sure everyone is included.

Still, there are concerns. Many people, liberal and conservative, fear that a system with multiple insurance companies can never succeed because of efforts that insurers make to tilt their mix of enrollees. We do not know if our efforts to combat this selection will work well enough. This concern is legitimate; people who believe it strongly support single-payer systems.

An additional concern is the potential adverse economic effects of such a system. The tax credits proposed here are higher for the poor, and become smaller as income rises. Will the fact that increased income reduces the tax credit one receives lead people to work less or save less? Economists term these effects deadweight losses, economically unproductive actions people take in response to taxation. Deadweight losses that are too big can make otherwise valuable programs not worth it.

There will certainly be such effects for some people. But there will be offsetting benefits as well. Allowing people to change jobs without worry of losing health insurance will reduce some current labor market distortions. Further, universal coverage will remove the incentive some families have to keep incomes low in order to qualify for Medicaid. These benefits offset the potential costs from phasing out the tax credit.

There are no good estimates of the net cost or benefit in economic activity of moving to a system of universal insurance coverage. The best we can do is design the most efficient possible system. The one proposed here has the fewest distortions.

The history of health reform in the United States is not encouraging of efforts to guarantee universal insurance. President Theodore Roosevelt supported universal health insurance when he ran on the Bull Moose party in 1912, but he was not elected. Franklin Roosevelt considered including national health insurance as part of Social Security in the 1930s but decided not to push it. Proposals for universal insurance coverage were put forward by Harry Truman in the 1940s, Richard Nixon and Jimmy Carter in the 1970s, and Bill Clinton in the 1990s. None of them succeeded.

Specific interest groups will always oppose publicly financed coverage expansions. Unions led the charge against the earliest attempts at universal coverage, viewing health insurance as a matter for workers and employers; today, organized labor is among the most ardent supporters of universal insurance. The American Medical Association was the chief foe of national insurance early in the post-World War II era, fearing it would limit physician incomes. The medical establishment now supports expanded coverage. The Clinton plan was opposed by (among others) health insurers, who feared the plan's restrictions on their business: small businesses, who were worried about the economic effects of mandated employer payments: and antitax crusaders, who worried about the effect of government's taking on a major new commitment. Some of these groups may oppose the plan I put forward, although the opposition will be less vehement without the mandated employer payments and heavy regulatory apparatus.

But the opposition of specific interests does not explain the continued failure of politicians to enact universal coverage. There have been too many skilled politicians who have failed at the task of instituting universal insurance simply to blame opposing interest groups. The problem is deeper. I believe that the real reason health care reform has not succeeded is rooted in a misconception of what health care reform should accomplish. Almost all health care reform proposals presume two problems: the need for universal insurance coverage; and the need to control medical costs. We want to insure everyone, but we have to save money in the existing system as well. Seen this way, there is but one solution: Limit the growth of medical costs, and use the savings to pay for expanded insurance coverage.

The difficulty with this approach is apparent in its formulation: It is great that more people will be covered because of health care reform, but who will volunteer to sacrifice their own care to achieve this? Health care reform became synonymous with rationing. Of course, this is not a fair characterization. There is waste in the system, and the goal of most reformers is to lower spending by eliminating that waste. But there is no guarantee that the services eliminated by cost cutting will be the wasteful ones. People with insurance fear that their care will be made worse so that others can have insurance coverage. It is not a winning strategy.

Fundamentally, this reflects a failure of our public sector to grasp the essential issues. Cost containment is not a goal in itself. Increasing the value of the system is. The right step is to move toward a system that improves our health, spending less as appropriate but more if need be. We can move forward on this, but we must think differently than we have.

Notes

Introduction: Crisis by Design

1. Karen Donelan et al., "The Cost of Health System Change: Public Discontent in Five Nations," *Health Affairs* 18, no. 3 (1999), 206–16.
2. "Rising Health Costs Signal Ominous Emerging Trend," *USA Today*, April 22, 2002, p. 11A.
3. Ceci Connelly, "Health-Care Costs Jump at Calpers; Big Premium Increase May Signal Trend," *Washington Post*, April 17, 2002, p. E1.
4. The expert was Walter Zelman, head of the California Association for Health Plans. See Victoria Colliver, "CalPERS Health Costs to Rise," *San Francisco Chronicle*, April 13, 2002, p. A1.
5. Institute of Medicine, *Care Without Coverage: Too Little, Too Late* (Washington, D.C.: National Academy Press, 2002), Appendix D, 162.
6. Institute of Medicine, *To Err Is Human: Building a Safer Medical System* (Washington, D.C.: National Academy Press, 2000), 1.

1 The Health of the Nation: A History

1. Good data on longevity in the United States have been available since about 1900. This is relatively late by international standards; France and England have much longer data records. But the patterns before 1900 are likely similar to those after. For more information on long-term trends, see Robert W. Fogel, "Economic Growth, Population Theory, and Physiology: The Bearing of Long-Term Processes on the Making of Economic Policy," *American Economic Review* (June 1994): 369–95.
2. A century earlier, life expectancy at birth was probably about 35 years.
3. David Cutler and Ellen Meara, "Changes in the Age Distribution of Mortality Over the 20th Century," in David Wise, ed., *Perspectives on the Economics of Aging*, Chicago: University of Chicago Press, 1993.

4. Albert Bergeron, as quoted in *Perspectives on the Economics of Aging*, ed. David Wise (Chicago: University of Chicago Press, forthcoming).

5. Fogel, "Economic Growth, Population Theory, and Physiology"; and Sam Preston,."American Longevity: Past, Present, and Future," Syracuse University Policy Brief No. 7/1996, Distinguished Lecturer in Aging Series, Center for Economic Policy Research Policy Brief, 1996.

6. René Dubos, "The Diseases of Civilizations," *Milbank Memorial Fund Quarterly* 47 (1969): 327–29.

7. For an excellent history of medicine, see Paul Starr, *The Social Transformation of American Medicine* (New York: Basic Books, 1982).

8. The medical education system was partly to blame. In 1910 Abraham Flexner wrote a famous report on medical schools documenting that they did not have many promised courses, had poorly trained or no faculty, and admitted students who were not prepared. Abraham Flexner, *Medical Education in the United States and Canada*, Bulletin No. 4 (New York: Carnegie Foundation for the Advancement of Teaching, 1910). Fortunately, many of these schools merged or folded in the next few decades.

9. Judith Walzer Leavitt, "Politics and Public Health: Smallpox in Milwaukee, 1894–95," in *Health Care in America: Essays in Social History*, ed. Susan Reverby and David Rosner (Philadelphia: Temple University Press, 1979), 84–101.

10. Within nonsurgical medicine, for example, there were recognized subspecialties only in cardiovascular disease, gastroenterology, and pulmonary disease. Not yet invented were endocrinology (1971), hematology (1971), medical oncology (1972), and critical care medicine (1985), to name a few. The first surgical subspecialties were not recognized until the 1970s. All surgeons did all operations.

11. Vannevar Bush, *Science: The Endless Frontier* (Washington, D.C.: Government Printing Office, 1945), chap. 2.

12. Quoted in Henry E. Sigerist, *Landmarks in the History of Hygiene* (London: Oxford University Press, 1956), 50–51. See also Herman Freudenberger and Gaylord Cummins, "Health, Work, and Leisure before the Industrial Revolution," *Explorations in Economic History* 13, no. 1 (January 1976): 1–12.

13. Freudenberger and Cummins, "Health, Work, and Leisure before the Industrial Revolution," 8.

14. William Osler, "Valedictory Address at Johns Hopkins University," *Journal of the American Medical Association* 44 (1905): 706.

15. Before Social Security was introduced in the 1930s, the Civil War pension was the most extensive retirement program in the United States. Begun in 1862, the pension system lasted into the twentieth century. Health assessments were an integral part of the program; more was paid to people with greater disability. These health records have survived and

were painstakingly assembled for analysis by economist Robert Fogel of the University of Chicago. Fogel has analyzed the data with Dora Costa of MIT.

16. These data were graciously provided by the United States American Track Foundation, Road Running Information Center.

17. Dora Costa, *The Evolution of Retirement: An American Economic History 1880–1990* (Chicago: University of Chicago Press, 1998).

18. See, for example, Lois M. Verbrugge, "Recent, Present, and Future Health of American Adults," in *Annual Review of Public Health,* vol. 10, ed. Lester Breslow, Jonathan E. Fielding, and Lester B. Lave (Palo Alto: Annual Reviews, 1989); and Eileen M. Crimmins and Dominique G. Ingegneri, "Trends in the Health of the U.S. Population: 1957–1989," in *The State of Humanity,* ed. Julian Simon (Cambridge, Mass.: Blackwell, 1995), 72–84.

19. In later chapters I show that disease diagnosis almost always increases when the ability to treat disease improves.

20. Timothy Waidmann, John Bound, and Michael Schoenbaum, "The Illusion of Failure," *Milbank Quarterly* 73, no. 2 (June 1995): 253–88.

21. The most notable of these studies is the National Long-Term Care Survey. See Kenneth G. Manton and Xuliang Gu, "Changes in the Prevalence of Chronic Disability in the United States Black and Nonblack Population above Age 65 from 1982 to 1999," *Proceedings of the National Academy of Sciences* 98, no. 12 (June 5, 2001): 6354–59.

22. For a summary of surveys and measures, see David Cutler, "Declining Disability among the Elderly," *Health Affairs* 20, no. 6 (November/December 2001): 11–27.

23. Recently, there has been a more concerted effort to measure mental health, as concern about this aspect of health has increased. Surveys of mental health were conducted in the early 1980s and early 1990s; followups are ongoing. But the results are less consistent than are those of surveys on physical disability. Definitions of mental illness have changed even in the past two decades, and the responses that people give have fundamental inconsistencies. For the controversy about changes in mental health, see Darrel A. Regier et al., "Limitations of Diagnostic Criteria and Assessment Instruments for Mental Disorders: Implications for Research and Policy," *Archives of General Psychiatry* 55, no. 2 (February 1998): 109–15; and Gerald L. Klerman and Myrna M. Weissman, "Increasing Rates of Depression," *Journal of the American Medical Association* 261, no. 15 (April 21, 1989): 2229–35.

2 Pricing the Priceless

1. The title for this chapter is taken from Joseph P. Newhouse, *Pricing the Priceless* (Cambridge: MIT Press, 2002).

2. Deut. 34:7.

3. Daniel Callahan, *False Hopes: Why America's Quest for Perfect Health is a Recipe for Failure,* manuscript in preparation.

4. For a summary of various approaches to valuing health, see Michael Walzer, *Spheres of Justice: A Defense of Pluralism and Equality* (New York: Basic Books, 1983); Amartya Sen, *Commodities and Capabilities* (New Delhi: Oxford University Press, 1999); Norman Daniels, *Just Health-Care* (Cambridge: Cambridge University Press, 1991); Amy Gutmann and Dennis Thompson, "Why Deliberative Democracy is Different," *Social Philosophy and Policy* 17 (2000): 161–80; Jill Horwitz, "Why We Need the Independent Sector: The Behavior, Law, and Ethics of Not-for-Profit Hospitals," *UCLA Law Review,* forthcoming.

5. Alexander Volokh, "n Guilty Men," *University of Pennsylvania Law Review* 146 (1997): 173–216, is an amusing and quite informative look at this question.

6. William Blackstone, *Commentaries on the Laws of England* 4 (1772; reprint, Chicago: University of Chicago Press, 2002).

7. Sir William Petty, *Political Arhithmetick* (1691) in *The Economic Writings of Sir William Petty,* ed. C. H. Hull (Cambridge: Cambridge University Press, 1899). See also Rashi Fein, "On Measuring Economic Benefits of Health Programmes," in *Medical History and Medical Care,* ed. Gordon McLachlan and Thomas McKeown (London: Oxford University Press, 1971), 181–217.

8. Many oppose this procedure on philosophical grounds. Deciding that health is an aggregation of individual preferences denies some of the specialness of health. There might be some conditions that people do not value so highly but for other reasons we as a society might value extremely highly (curing people who have diseases that are entirely beyond their fault, for example). Still, determining the average value is the most fruitful way to proceed.

9. The term QALY was coined by Richard Zeckhauser and Donald Shepard, "Where Now for Saving Lives?" *Law and Contemporary Problems* 40, no. 4 (1976): 5–45. Zeckhauser relates that his first suggestion for the term was "quality-adjusted citizen years," to reflect the fact that all people count equally. Fortunately, QACYs was rejected in favor of QALYs.

10. These estimates are from John D. Graham et al., "The Cost-Effectiveness of Air Bags by Seating Position," *Journal of the American Medical Association* 278, no. 17 (November 5, 1997): 1418–25. They estimate that air bags reduce auto fatalities by ten persons per one million vehicles. If an air bag lasts ten years, this is about a hundred persons per one million vehicle years, or a one in ten thousand chance of survival. Air bags also reduce injury, but the example is clearest considering only mortality.

11. In economics, this is termed a willingness-to-pay study. A related methodology, termed willingness to accept, looks at how much people need to be compensated to accept a greater health risk.

12. W. Kip Viscusi, "The Value of Risks to Life and Health," *Journal of Economic Literature* 31, (December 1993): 1912–46; and George S. Tolley, Donald S. Kenkel, and Robert G. Fabian, eds., *Valuing Health for Policy: An Economic Approach* (Chicago: University of Chicago Press, 1994).

13. William Nordhaus, "The Health of Nations: The Contribution of Improved Health to Living Standards," in *Measuring the Gains from Medical Research: An Economic Approach*, ed. Kevin Murphy and Robert Topel (Chicago: University of Chicago Press, 2003).

14. As noted above, this is not without dispute. The utilitarian approach judges all health interventions as morally equivalent. This need not be the case.

15. For a discussion of quality-adjusted life years, see John Harris, "QALY-fying the Value of Life," *Journal of Medical Ethics* 13, no. 3 (September 1987): 117–23. For a general discussion of approaches, see Richard H. Morrow and John H. Bryant, "Health Policy Approaches to Measuring and Valuing Human Life: Conceptual and Ethical Issues," *American Journal of Public Health* 85, no. 10 (October 1995): 1356–60.

16. Our initial data went through the mid-1990s. We have subsequently expanded the data through the late 1990s. The conclusions are similar for both time periods. For completeness, I report results over the entire time period.

17. David M. Cutler et al., "Are Medical Prices Falling?" *Quarterly Journal of Economics* (November 1998): 991–1024. The updated analysis is in David M. Cutler and Mark McClellan, "Is Technological Change in Medicine Worth It?" *Health Affairs* 20, no. 5 (September/October 2001): 11–29.

3 Success and Failure at the Beginning of Life

1. This story is told in Douglas K. Richardson, "A Woman with an Extremely Premature Newborn," *Journal of the American Medical Association* 286, no. 12 (September 26, 2001): 1498–1505.

2. Infant mortality has declined throughout the developed world. See Carlo A. Corsini and Pier Paolo Viazzo, *The Decline of Infant and Child Mortality: The European Experience, 1750–1990*, (Boston: Klewer, 1997).

3. Clement A. Smith, "Physiologic Basis of High Humidity in the Prevention of Neonatal Morbidity," *New York State Journal of Medicine* 55 (1955): 2051.

4. David Cutler and Ellen Meara, "The Technology of Birth: Is It Worth It?" in *Frontiers in Health Policy Research*, vol. 3, ed. Alan Garber (Cambridge: MIT Press, 2000), 33–67. The details of the statistical analysis in this chapter can be found in that paper, or in the technical appendix.

5. It is not known what the care of adults who were born disabled, low-birth-weight infants will cost. To be conservative, I assume they need a lot of care.

6. An older survey is that of Maureen Hack, Nancy K. Klein, and H. Gerry

Taylor, "Long-Term Developmental Outcomes of Low Birth Weight Infants," *The Future of Children* 5, no. 1 (Spring 1995): 176–96. A more recent study by Maureen Hack and colleagues, looking at very low-birth-weight infants around age 20, found that only 10 percent had neurosensory impairments. Indeed, on some dimensions, quality of life was better for the low-birth-weight infants than for the normal-birth-weight infants. Maureen Hack et al., "Outcomes in Young Adulthood for Very-Low-Birth-Weight Infants," *New England Journal of Medicine* 346, no. 3 (January 17, 2002): 149–57.

7. One drawback of the data that is worth mentioning is that the older data have information on birth weight but not gestational age. Medical advance should really be identified from birth weight and gestation age-specific mortality. In practice, though, gestational age is difficult to measure accurately. Further, birth weight and gestational age are very highly correlated. Thus, most researchers look only at birth weight. We did the same.

8. David J. P. Barker, *Mothers, Babies, and Health in Later Life*, 2nd ed. (London: Churchill Livingstone, 1998). This is likely caused by developmental problems resulting from inadequate nutrition in utero.

9. Saroj Saigal et al., "Self-Perceived Health Status and Health-Related Qualify of Life of Extremely Low Birth Weight Infants at Adolescence," *Journal of the American Medical Association* 276, no. 6 (August 14, 1996): 453–59; Saroj Sagal et al., "Parental Perspectives of the Health Status and Health-Related Quality of Life of Teen-Aged Children Who Were Extremely Low Birth Weight and Term Controls," *Pediatrics* 105, no. 3 (March 2000): 569–74.

10. At the high end, special education and disability costs are $25,000 per infant. On average, spending is $10,000 per infant. Thirteen years of life valued at about $90,000 per year would be about $1 million. Taking into account of the fact that many of the years are lived in the future lowers the benefits to $350,000 per infant.

11. For reviews of the literature, see John G. Frohna, Paula M. Lantz, and Harold Pollack, "Maternal Substance Abuse and Infant Health: Policy Options across the Life Course," *Milbank Quarterly* 77, no. 4 (1999): 531–70, and R. Louise Floyd et al., "A Review of Smoking in Pregnancy: Effects on Pregnancy Outcomes and Cessation Efforts," *Annual Review of Public Health* 14 (1993): 379–411.

12. James S. Marks et al., "A Cost-Benefit/Cost-Effectiveness Analysis of Smoking Cessation for Pregnant Women," *American Journal of Preventive Medicine* 6, no. 5 (1990): 282–89.

13. Institute of Medicine, *Preventing Low Birth Weight* (Washington, D.C.: National Academy of Sciences, 1985).

14. David Cutler and Jonathan Gruber, "The Effect of Medicaid Expansions

on Public Insurance, Private Insurance, and Redistribution," *American Economic Review* 86, no. 2 (May 1996): 378–83.

15. David Cutler and Jonathan Gruber, "Does Public Insurance Crowd Out Private Insurance?" *Quarterly Journal of Economics* 111, no. 2 (May 1996): 391–430.

16. Hospitals were allowed to enroll people when they showed up and to receive payment for the services just provided. See Joyce M. Piper, Wayne A. Ray, and Marie R. Griffin, "Effects of Medicaid Eligibility Expansion on Prenatal Care and Pregnancy Outcomes in Tennessee," *Journal of the American Medical Association* 264, no. 22 (November 7, 1990): 2219–23.

17. Janet Currie and Jonathan Gruber, "Health Insurance Eligibility, Utilization of Medical Care, and Child Health," *Quarterly Journal of Economics* 111, no. 2 (May 1996): 431–66; Janet Currie and Jonathan Gruber, "Saving Babies: The Efficacy and Cost of Recent Expansions of Medicaid Eligibility for Pregnant Women," *Journal of Political Economy* 104, no. 6 (December 1996): 1263–96.

4 The Power of the Pill

1. Melanie Thernstrom, *Halfway Heaven* (New York: Doubleday, 1997).

2. The prevalence of mental illness and spending on mental illness is taken from U.S. Surgeon General, *Mental Health: A Report of the Surgeon General*, Department of Health and Human Services, 1999. That report is an excellent summary of mental health diagnosis and treatment. Suicide rates are from the Centers for Disease Control and Prevention, *Vital Statistics*, 2001.

3. For a history of views about the mentally ill and changes in the psychiatric profession, see Gerald N. Grob, *From Asylum to Community: Mental Health Policy in Modern America* (Princeton: Princeton University Press, 1991).

4. Statistics on the prevalence of mental illness are also from the Surgeon General's *Mental Health* report.

5. For description and summary of depression in particular, see Kenneth Wells and Roland Sturm, *Caring for Depression* (Cambridge: Harvard University Press, 1996). Many of the descriptive facts in this chapter can be found in that book and the references therein.

6. The National Comorbidity Study estimates that several million more adults suffer from depression.

7. The figures in this paragraph come from Paul E. Greenberg et al., "The Economic Burden of Depression in 1990," *Journal of Clinical Psychiatry* 54 (1993): 405–18; and Ernst R. Berndt et al., "Lost Human Capital from Early Onset Chronic Depression," *American Journal of Psychiatry* 157, no.

6 (June 2000): 940–47. Mental health spending as a whole is much greater than just the $12 billion.

8. Dorothy P. Rice, "Economic Burden of Mental Disorders in the United States," *Economics of Neuroscience* 1, no. 2 (1999): 40–4; and Paul E. Greenberg, Stephanie A. Leong, and Howard G. Birnbaum, "Cost of Depression: Current Assessment and Future Directions," *Expert Review of Pharmacoeconomics and Outcomes Research* 1, no. 1 (2001): 69–76.

9. The Surgeon General's *Mental Health* report and Wells and Sturm, *Caring for Depression,* discuss this issue. Historically, some mental illnesses were associated with infections, such as neurosyphilis (an outgrowth of syphilis), but that is not believed to be the case now.

10. See Grob, *From Asylum to Community,* and David Healy, *The Antidepressant Era* (Cambridge: Harvard University Press, 1998) for excellent discussions of treatment changes.

11. The quotation is taken from PBS, *A Brilliant Madness,* primary source material, located at http://www.pbs.org/wgbh/amex/nash/filmmore/ps_ict.html (June 4, 2002).

12. For a history of the development of antidepressant medications, see Healy, *The Antidepressant Era.*

13. While such a theoretical distinction dated back to the end of the nineteenth century, it wasn't until treatment became differentiated that clinicians found the distinction useful.

14. The success of imipramine spawned many similar compounds, including amitriptyline, nortriptyline, desipramine, and protriptyline.

15. For a review, see Robert M. Hirschfeld et al., "The National Depressive and Manic-Depressive Association Consensus Statement on the Undertreatment of Depression," *Journal of the American Medical Association* 277, no. 4 (January 22/29, 1997): 333–40.

16. Lee N. Robins, Ben Z. Locke, and Darrel A. Regier, "An Overview of Psychiatric Disorders in America," in *Psychiatric Disorders in America: The Epidemiological Catchment Area Study,* ed. Lee N. Robins and Darrel A. Regier (New York: Free Press, 1991), 328–66. Other studies place effective treatment rates at 5 to 25 percent.

17. Martin B. Keller, Gerald L. Klerman, and Philip W. Lavori, "Treatment Received by Depressed Patients," *Journal of the American Medical Association* 248 (1982): 1848–55; Martin B. Keller et al., "Treatment for Chronic Depression with Sertraline and Imipramine: Preliminary Blinded Response Rate and High Rates of Undertreatment in the Community," *Psychopharmacology Bulletin* 31 (1995): 205–12; James H. Kocsis et al., "Imipramine Treatment for Chronic Depression," *Archives of General Psychiatry* 45 (1988): 253–57; James H. Kocsis et al., "Maintenance Therapy for Chronic Depression: A Controlled Trial of Desipramine," *Archives of General Psychiatry* 53 (1996): 769–74; Richard C. Shelton et al., "The

Undertreatment of Dysthymia," *Journal of Clinical Psychiatry* 58 (1997): 59–65. For discussion, see Jonathan R. T. Davidson and Samantha E. Meltzer-Brody, "The Underrecognition and Undertreatment of Depression: What is the Breadth and Depth of the Problem?" *Journal of Clinical Psychiatry* 60, Supp. 7 (1999): 4–9.

18. David P. Goldberg and Barry Blackwell, "Psychiatric Illness in General Practice: A Detailed Study Using a New Method of Case Identification," *British Medical Journal* 2 (1970): 439–43; J. N. Marks, David P. Goldberg, and V. F. Hillier, "Determinants of the Ability of General Practitioners to Detect Psychiatric Illness," *Psychological Medicine* 9 (1979): 337–53.

19. Janet Hankin and Julianne S. Oktay, *Mental Disorder and Primary Medical Care: An Analytical Review of the Literature*, Series D. No. 5 (Washington, D.C.: National Institutes of Mental Health, 1979).

20. Data on the efficacy of treatment for depression are from Agency for Health Care Policy and Research, *Depression in Primary Care, Vol. 2: Treatment of Major Depression*, Clinical Practice Guideline No. 5 (Washington, D.C.: AHCPR, April 1993), AHCPR Publication No. 93–0551; and American Psychiatric Association, "Practice Guidelines for Major Depressive Disorder in Adults," *American Journal of Psychiatry* 150, no. 4, Supp. (April 1993): 1–26. Shortly after Prozac was first marketed, a report by Martin Teicher of Harvard Medical School reported increased suicidal ideation in six people taking Prozac (Martin Teicher, Carol Glod, and Jonathan O. Cole, "Emergence of Intense Suicidal Preoccupation During Fluoxetine Treatment," *American Journal of Psychiatry* 147, no. 2 [February 1990]: 207–10). This made headlines, just as had the approval of Prozac. Reviews of larger numbers of patients did not support the finding, however. Rather, it is believed that the suicidal thoughts some people experience as they take any antidepressant medication are a result of the underlying depression, not the treatment. The claim that Prozac leads to suicidal or other harmful impulses has recently been suggested again, most prominently by psychiatrist Joseph Glenmullen in *Prozac Backlash* (New York: Simon and Schuster, 2000), but the clinical literature has so far not supported such claims.

21. Michael E. Thase et al., "Treatment of Major Depression with Psychotherapy or Psychotherapy-Pharmacotherapy Combinations," *Archives of General Psychiatry* 54, no. 11 (November 1997): 1009–15.

22. Some patients taking SSRIs experience moderate side effects such as gastrointestinal symptoms (nausea and diarrhea), headache, insomnia, anxiety, and sexual dysfunction. But overall the symptoms are milder than with TCAs. Also, the potentially fatal cardiovascular consequences of overdose are not present.

23. Prozac's patent expired in 2002. Generic versions are now available at much lower prices.

24. Bernice A. Pescosolido et al., *Americans' View of Mental Health and Illness at Century's End: Continuity and Change* (Bloomington: Indiana Consortium for Mental Health Services Research, 2000).

25. These data are from the National Ambulatory Medical Care Survey, described in the technical appendix.

26. Thomas Croghan, "The Controversy of Increased Spending for Antidepressants," *Health Affairs* 20, no. 2 (March/April 2001): 129–35; Veronica V. Goff, "Depression: A Decade of Progress, More to Do," National Health Policy Forum Issue Brief No. 786, November 22, 2002.

27. See Richard G. Frank, Susan H. Busch, and Ernst R. Berndt, "Measuring Prices and Quantities of Treatment for Depression," *American Economic Review* 88, no. 2 (May 1998): 106–11; Richard G. Frank, Ernst R. Berndt, and Susan H. Busch, "Price Indexes for the Treatment of Depression," in *Measuring the Prices of Medical Treatments*, ed. Jack Triplett (Washington, D.C.: The Brookings Institution, 1998); Richard G. Frank et al., "The Value of Mental Health Care at the System Level: The Case of Treating Depression," *Health Affairs* 18, no. 5 (September/October 1999): 71–88; Ernst R. Berndt et al., "The Medical Treatment of Depression, 1991–1996: Productive Inefficiency, Expected Outcome Variations, and Price Indexes," *Journal of Health Economics* 21, no. 3 (May 2002): 373–96; and Ernst R. Berndt, Susan H. Busch, and Richard G. Frank, "Price Indexes for Acute Phase Treatment of Depression," in *Medical Care Output and Productivity*, ed. David Cutler and Ernst Berndt (Chicago: University of Chicago Press, 2001), 463–505.

28. David L. Sackett and George W. Torrence, "The Utility of Different Health States as Perceived by the General Public," *Journal of Chronic Diseases* 31, no. 11 (1978): 697–704; Dennis G. Frybeck et al., "The Beaver Dam Health Outcomes Study: Initial Catalog of Health-State Quality Factors," *Medical Decision Making* 13, no. 2 (April–June 1993): 89–102; Susan F. Anton and Dennis A. Revicki, "The Use of Decision Analysis in the Pharmacoeconomic Evaluation of an Antidepressant: A Cost-Effectiveness Study of Nefazodone," *Psychopharmacology Bulletin* 31, no. 2 (1995): 249–58; Christopher J. L. Murray and Alan D. Lopez, eds., *The Global Burden of Disease: a comprehensive assessment of mortality and disability from diseases, injuries, and risk factors in 1990 and projected to 2020* (Cambridge: Harvard University Press, 1996).

29. There are other benefits too. Younger people are more likely to finish their education when depression is treated, which should be factored in. Suicide might also be reduced. The literature does not have precise estimates of these effects, however. Thus, I do not factor them in. The technical appendix discusses the estimates I make.

30. Very few research studies examine this question. Those that do often look at physician-listed diagnoses for those taking antidepressants. Phy-

sicians who diagnose depression may not write down the appropriate code, however, because they are unfamiliar with the precise codes, or because they want to avoid a depression stigma for their patients. As a result, the research literature does not consider the reported diagnosis of someone taking antidepressant medication to be very relevant.

31. Ronald C. Kessler, et al., "The Epidemiology of Major Depressive Disorder: Results from the National Comorbidity Survey Replication (NCS-R)", *Journal of the American Medical Association* 289, no. 23 (June 18, 2003): 3095–3105; Alexander S. Young et al., "The Quality of Care for Depressive and Anxiety Disorders in the United States," *Archives of General Psychiatry* 58, no. 1 (January 2001): 55–61; Philip S. Wang, Patricia Berglund, and Ronald C. Kessler, "Recent Care of Common Mental Disorders in the United States," *Journal of General Internal Medicine* 15, no. 5 (May 2000): 284–92.

32. Two studies investigate this issue. Philip S. Wang, Patricia Berglund, and Ronald C. Kessler, in "Recent Care of Common Mental Disorders in the United States," show significant effects of health insurance on any use of care and use of appropriate care. Alexander S. Young et al., "The Quality of Care for Depressive and Anxiety Disorders in the United States," estimates that insurance affects the probability of receiving care, but not whether those who received care were treated at guideline levels.

33. Kathryn J. Aiken, "Direct-to-Consumer Advertising of Prescription Drugs: Physician Survey, Preliminary Results," United States Food and Drug Administration, January 2003.

5 The Heart of the Matter

1. For discussion of Roosevelt's illness and its implications, see Robert H. Ferrell, *The Dying President: Franklin D. Roosevelt, 1944–45* (Columbia: University of Missouri Press, 1998); Franz H. Messerli, "Occasional Notes: This Day 50 Years Ago," *New England Journal of Medicine* 332, no. 15 (April 13, 1995): 1038–39; Ray W. Gifford, "FDR and Hypertension: If We'd Only Known Then What We Know Now," *Geriatrics* 51 (January 1996): 29–32; Alvan L. Barach, "Franklin Roosevelt's Illness: Effect on Course of History," *New York State Journal of Medicine* 77, no. 13 (November 1977): 2154–57; Jeffrey Hart, "While America Slept," *National Review*, September 15, 1989, 32–34.

2. Lord Moran, *Winston Churchill: The Struggle for Survival, 1940–1965* (London: The Chaucer Press, 1966), 223.

3. Howard G. Bruenn, "Clinical Notes on the Illness and Death of President Franklin D. Roosevelt," *Annals of Internal Medicine* 72 (1970): 591.

4. The research in this chapter is explained in more detail in the technical appendix.

5. For a longer rendition, see Eugene Braumwald, "Evolution of the

Management of Acute Myocardial Infarction: A 20th Century Saga," *The Lancet* 352, no. 9142 (November 8, 1998): 1771–74.

6. Henry A. Christian, ed., *The Principles and Practice of Medicine, Originally Written by William Osler*, 16th ed. (New York: D. Appleton-Century, 1947).

7. For more discussion of Eisenhower's heart attack, including the claim that Eisenhower's physician misdiagnosed the heart attack in the crucial first few hours, see Clarence G. Lasby, *Eisenhower's Heart Attack* (Lawrence: University of Kansas Press, 1997). Winston Churchill nearly received the same therapy. Churchill's physician suspected that he had had a heart attack in December 1941, just after the United States entered World War II. But the doctor told no one. There was little he could do, and besides, "The textbook treatment for this is at least six weeks in bed. That would mean publishing to the world—and the American newspapers would see to this [Churchill was in Washington at the time]—that the P.M. was an invalid with a crippled heart and a doubtful future. And this at a moment when America has just come into the war, and there is no one but Winston to take her by the hand. I felt that the effect of announcing that the P.M. had had a heart attack could only be disastrous. . . . Right or wrong, it seemed plain that I must sit tight on what had happened, whatever the consequences." Lord Moran, *Winston Churchill: The Struggle for Survival, 1940–1965*, 16–17. Fortunately, it is unlikely that Churchill had truly had a heart attack.

8. There is now some non-acute usage of these therapies, but that was uncommon until very recently.

9. U.S. Public Health Service, *High Blood Pressure* (Washington, D.C.: Government Printing Office, 1948).

10. The earliest results from the Framingham Heart Study are in William B. Kannel et al., "Factors of Risk in the Development of Coronary Heart Disease—Six Year Follow-up Experience; the Framingham Study," *Annals of Internal Medicine* 55 (1961): 33–50.

11. Veterans Administration Cooperative Study Group on Antihypertensive Agents, "Effects of Treatment on Morbidity in Hypertension: Results in Patients with Diastolic Pressures Averaging 115 through 129 mm Hg," *Journal of the American Medical Association* 202, no. 11 (December 11, 1967): 1028–34; Veterans Administration Cooperative Study Group on Antihypertensive Agents, "Effects of Treatment on Morbidity in Hypertension: Results in Patients with Diastolic Pressures Averaging 90 through 114 mm Hg," *Journal of the American Medical Association* 213, no. 7 (August 17, 1970): 1143–52.

12. Ancel Keys, *Coronary Heart Disease in Seven Countries* (New York: American Heart Association, 1970).

13. Trends in hypertension are presented in Vicki L. Burt et al., "Trends in the Prevalence, Awareness, Treatment, and Control of Hypertension in

the Adult US Population," *Hypertension* 26, no. 1 (July 1995): 60–69. Trends in high cholesterol are presented in Christopher T. Sempos et al., "Prevalence of High Blood Cholesterol Among US Adults: An Update Based on Guidelines from the Second Report of the National Cholesterol Education Program Adult Treatment Panel," *Journal of the American Medical Association* 269, no. 23 (June 16, 1993): 3009–14.

14. Lee Goldman et al., "The Effect of Risk Factor Reductions between 1981 and 1990 on Coronary Heart Disease Incidence, Prevalence, Mortality and Cost," *Journal of the American College of Cardiology* 38, no. 4 (October 2001): 1012–17.

15. Pauline M. Ippolito and Alan D. Mathios, *Information and Advertising Policy: A Study of Fat and Cholesterol Consumption in the United States, 1977–1990* (Washington, D.C.: Federal Trade Commission, 1996); Alison M. Stephen and Nicholas J. Wald, "Trends in Individual Consumption of Dietary Fat in the United States, 1920-1984," *American Journal of Clinical Nutrition* 52, no. 3 (September 1990): 457–69.

16. Alta Engstrom, Rosemary C. Tobelmann, and Ann M. Albertson, "Sodium Intake Trends and Food Choices," *American Journal of Clinical Nutrition* 65, no. 2, Supp. (February 1997): 704S–7S.

17. David Cutler, Edward Glaeser, and Jesse Shapiro, "Why Are Americans More Obese?" forthcoming in *Journal of Economic Perspectives* 17, no. 3 (Summer 2003).

18. Information on obesity may be found in Robert J. Kuczmarski et al., "Increasing Prevalence of Overweight Among US Adults," *Journal of the American Medical Association* 272, no. 3 (July 20, 1994): 205–11. Data on diabetes are in Maureen I. Harris et al., "Prevalence of Diabetes, Impaired Fasting Glucose, and Impaired Glucose Tolerance in U.S. Adults: The Third National Health and Nutrition Examination Survey, 1988–1994," *Diabetes Care* 21, no. 4 (April 1998): 518–24.

19. This is the premise of the "Atkins," or low-carbohydrate, diet.

20. Julian P. Midgley et al., "Effect of Reduced Dietary Sodium on Blood Pressure: A Meta-Analysis of Randomized Controlled Trials," *Journal of the American Medical Association* 275, no. 20 (May 22, 1996): 1590–96.

21. Evidence on the role of diet in hypertension comes from the DASH study (Dietary Approach to Stopping Hypertension): DASH Collaborative Research Group, "A Clinical Trial of the Effects of Dietary Patterns on Blood Pressure," *New England Journal of Medicine* 336, no. 16 (April 17, 1997): 1117–24.

22. Kishore J. Harjai, "Potential New Cardiovascular Disease Risk Factors: Left Ventricular Hypertrophy, Homocysteine, Lipoprotein(a), Triglycerides, Oxidative Stress, and Fibrinogen," *Annals of Internal Medicine* 131, no. 5 (September 7, 1999): 376–86.

23. Paul M. Ridker et al., "Inflammation, Aspirin, and the Risk of

Cardiovascular Disease in Apparently Healthy Men," *New England Journal of Medicine* 336, no. 14 (April 3, 1997): 973–79; Paul M. Ridker et al., "C-Reactive Protein and Other Markers of Inflammation in the Prediction of Cardiovascular Disease in Women," *New England Journal of Medicine* 342, no. 12 (March 23, 2000): 836–43; Paul M. Ridker et al., "Comparison of C-Reactive Protein and Low-density Lipoprotein Cholesterol Levels in the Prediction of First Cardiovascular Events," *New England Journal of Medicine*, 347, no. 20 (November 14, 2002): 1557–65.

24. Christine Espinola-Klein et al., "Impact of Infectious Burden on Extent and Long-Term Prognosis of Atherosclerosis," *Circulation* 105, no. 1 (January 1/8, 2002): 15–21; Stephen E. Epstein, "The Multiple Mechanisms by Which Infection May Contribute to Atherosclerosis Development and Course," *Circulation Research* 90, no. 1 (January 11, 2002): 2–4. Paul M. Ridker, "Inflammation, Infection, and Cardiovascular Risk: How Good is the Clinical Evidence?" *Circulation* 97, no. 17 (May 5, 1998): 1671–74.

25. *Chlamydia pneumoniae*, for example, is present in 70 to 80 percent of people aged 60 to 70; Cho-Chou Kuo, Lisa A. Jackson, Lee Ann Campbell, and J. Thomas, Grayston, *Chlamydia pneumoniae, Clinical Microbiology Review*, no. 8 (1995): 451–61; *Helicobacter pylori* is present in about 40 percent of middle aged men; Paul M. Ridker, John Danesh, Linda Youngman, Rory Collins, Meir J. Stampfer, Richard Peto, and Charles H. Hennekens, "A Prospective Study of *Helicobacter pylori* Seropositivity and the Risk for Future Myocardial Infarction among Socioeconomically Similar U.S. Men," *Annals of Internal Medicine*, no. 135 (2001): 184–88.

26. Paul M. Ridker, "Clinical Application of C-Reactive Protein for Cardiovascular Disease Detection and Prevention," *Circulation* 107, no. 3 (January 28, 2003): 363–69.

27. David J. P. Barker, *Mothers, Babies, and Health in Later Life* (Edinburgh: Churchill Livingstone, 1998).

28. Anita C. J. Ravelli et al., "Glucose Tolerance in Adults after Prenatal Exposure to the Dutch Famine," *Lancet* 351, no. 9097 (January 17, 1998): 173–77.

29. Gabriele Doblhammer and James W. Vaupel, "Lifespan Depends on Month of Birth," *Proceedings of the National Academy of Sciences* 98, no. 5 (February 27, 2001): 2934–39.

30. Data on birth weights early in the twentieth century are from Peter W. Ward, *Birth Weight and Economic Growth* (Chicago: University of Chicago Press, 1993); and Dora Costa, "Unequal At Birth: A Long-Term Comparison of Income and Birth Weight," *Journal of Economic History* 58, no. 4 (December 1998): 987–1009.

31. For an overview, see Robert M. Sapolsky, *Why Zebras Don't Get Ulcers* (New York: W. W. Freeman, 1998).

32. Michael G. Marmot, Martin J. Shipley, and Geoffrey Rose, "Inequalities

in Death—Specific Explanations of a General Pattern?" *Lancet* 1, no. 8384 (May 5, 1984): 1003–6; Michael G. Marmot, Manolis Kogevinas, and Maryann A. Elston, "Social/Economic Status and Disease," *Annual Review of Public Health* 8 (1987): 111–35.

33. Richard Wilkinson, *Unhealthy Societies* (London: Routledge, 1996). Other researchers have also contributed to this field. See Lisa F. Berkman, "The Role of Social Relations in Health Promotion," *Psychosomatic Medicine* 57, no. 3 (May-June 1995): 245–54.

34. Ken Judge, "Income Distribution and Life Expectancy: A Critical Appraisal," *British Medical Journal* 311, no. 7075 (November 11, 1995): 1282–85; Angus Deaton, "Relative Deprivation, Inequality, and Mortality," NBER Working Paper No. 8099, January 2001, unpublished. See also Wilkinson's response to Judge: Richard Wilkinson, "A Reply to Ken Judge," *British Medical Journal* 311, no. 7075 (November 11, 1995): 1285–87.

35. Lawrence F. Katz and Kevin Murphy, "Changes in Relative Wages, 1963–1987: Supply and Demand Factors," *Quarterly Journal of Economics* 107, no. 1 (1992): 35–78; Robert Putnam, *Bowling Alone* (New York: Touchstone Books, 2001).

36. For an attempt, see David Cutler et al., "Pricing Heart Attack Treatments," in *Medical Care Output and Productivity*, ed. David Cutler and Ernst Berndt (Chicago: University of Chicago Press, 2001), 305–62.

37. The exact increase is 4.4 years. The total increase in longevity for 45-year-olds was 4.7 years. The cardiovascular disease share is thus 85 percent.

38. A historical discussion of the link between cigarette smoking and disease is in *Reducing Tobacco Use: A Report of the Surgeon General* (Atlanta: U.S. Department of Health and Human Services, Office on Smoking and Health, 2000). Periodic tax increases and regulations on smoking have been important contributors, but less so than medical knowledge. More discussion on information provision and other factors is in David Cutler and Srikanth Kadiyala, "The Return to Biomedical Research: Treatment and Behavioral Effects," in *Measuring the Gains from Medical Research: An Economic Approach*, ed. Murphy and Topel.

39. The costs of public education are estimated in Lee Goldman et al., "The Effect of Risk Factor Reductions between 1981 and 1990 on Coronary Heart Disease Incidence, Prevalence, Mortality and Cost." They estimate costs at $3 per person per year, or perhaps $200 over a person's lifetime. A typical primary care visit costs about $50, so a few visits for information purposes is another $300 or so. This gives a total of $500.

40. There is an important quality of life component to the valuation here. In making behavioral changes, people have to give up something they like—smoking, high-fat food, or leisure, for example. This quality of life

reduction needs to be accounted for. Estimating the quality of life reduction associated with changing behavior is difficult for the same reasons that estimating the quality of life of anything is difficult; there are no market prices to look at. A benchmark estimate is that the quality reduction will be about half the value of the health improvement. The one-half calculation comes from economic reasoning. Suppose that I decide to cut back from one ice cream cone per day to an ice cream cone only on weekends, in an effort to improve my health. Giving up the first cone of the week has health benefits but low cost. After all, I still get plenty of ice cream. As I cut back more, the cost becomes increasingly larger, since there are more days in a row without ice cream. If I choose the amount of ice cream to give up optimally, the last cone foregone has quality of life costs exactly equal to the health benefits. The reason is simple. If giving up that ice cream has health benefits that are much greater than the value of the lost consumption, I would choose to give up even more—never to have ice cream again. Conversely, if the value of the last cone were much greater than the cost, I would not give it up. Now consider all the days of the week together. The first ice cream given up has only a small cost relative to the health benefits and the last cone given up has costs about equal to the benefits. The average quality of life cost is therefore about half the health benefits. Of course, nobody is that systematic (least of all about ice cream). But the reasoning gives a benchmark estimate; we can assume that the costs of behavioral change are about half of the health benefits.

41. John Z. Ayanian et al., "Unmet Health Needs of Uninsured Adults in the United States," *Journal of the American Medical Association* 284, no. 16 (October 25, 2000): 2061–69; Christine Huttin, John F. Moeller, and Randall S. Stafford, "Patterns and Costs for Hypertension Treatment in the United States," *Clinical Drug Investigation* 20, no. 3 (September 2000): 181–95; Cheryl Fish-Parcham, *Getting Less Care: The Uninsured with Chronic Health Conditions* (Washington, D.C.: Families USA Foundation, 2001); Gloria L. A. Beckles et al., "Population-Based Assessment of the Level of Care among Adults with Diabetes in the U.S.," *Diabetes Care* 21, no. 9 (September 1998): 1432–38; Joseph P. Newhouse and the Insurance Experiment Group, *Free for All: Lessons from the Rand Health Insurance Experiment* (Cambridge: Harvard University Press, 1993); Nicole Lurie et al., "Termination from Medi-Cal: Does It Affect Health?" *New England Journal of Medicine* 311, no. 7 (August 16, 1984): 480–84; Nicole Lurie et al., "Termination of Medi-Cal Benefits: A Followup Study One Year Later," *New England Journal of Medicine* 314, no. 19 (May 8, 1986): 1266–68.

42. Gary J. Young and Bruce B. Cohen, "Inequities in Hospital Care: The Massachusetts Experience," *Inquiry* 28, no. 3 (Fall 1991): 255–62; Jan

Blustein, Raymond R. Arons, and Steven Shea, "Sequential Events Contribution to Variations in Cardiac Revascularization Rates," *Medical Care* 33, no. 8 (August 1995): 864–80; Sylvia Kreindel et al., "Health Insurance Coverage and Outcome Following Acute Myocardial Infarction: A Community-Wide Perspective," *Archives of Internal Medicine* 157, no. 7 (April 14, 1997): 758–62; Mark J. Sada et al., "Influence of Payer on Use of Invasive Cardiac Procedures and Patient Outcome after Myocardial Infarction in the United States," *Journal of the American College of Cardiology* 31, no. 7 (June 1998): 1474–80; Lucien Leape et al., "Underuse of Cardiac Procedures: Do Women, Ethnic Minorities, and the Uninsured Fail to Receive Needed Revascularization?" *Annals of Internal Medicine* 130, no. 3 (February 2, 1999): 183–92; John G. Canto et al., "Payer Status and the Utilization of Hospital Resources in Acute Myocardial Infarction," *Archives of Internal Medicine* 160, no. 6 (March 27, 2000): 817–23.

43. Jack V. Tu et al., "Use of Cardiac Procedures and Outcomes in Elderly Patients with Myocardial Infarction in the United States and Canada," *New England Journal of Medicine* 336, no. 21 (May 22, 1997): 1500–5.

44. Jack V. Tu et al., "Use of Cardiac Procedures and Outcomes in Elderly Patients with Myocardial Infarction in the United States and Canada"; Jack V. Tu et al., "Coronary Artery Bypass Graft Surgery in Ontario and New York State: Which Rate Is Right?" *Annals of Internal Medicine* 126, no. 1 (January 1, 1997): 13–19. See also Jean L. Rouleau et al., "A Comparison of Management Patterns after Acute Myocardial Infarction in Canada and the United States," *New England Journal of Medicine* 328, no. 11 (March 18, 1993): 779–84; Daniel B. Mark, "Use of Medical Resources and Quality of Life after Acute Myocardial Infarction in Canada and the United States," *New England Journal of Medicine* 331, no. 17 (October 27, 1994): 1130–35; and Louise Pilote et al., "Differences in the Treatment of Myocardial Infarction in the United States and Canada," *Archives of Internal Medicine* 154, no. 10 (May 23, 1994): 1090–96. Different evidence is found by Anatoly Langer et al., "Higher Rates of Coronary Angiography and Revascularization Following Myocardial Infarction May Be Associated with Greater Survival in the United States Than in Canada," *Canadian Journal of Cardiology* 15, no. 10 (October 1999): 1095-1102.

45. Of course, survival isn't the only benefit of medical care. Cardiac surgery might improve quality of life as well. A few studies suggest that quality of life is higher in the United States than in Canada, possibly as a result of the higher surgery rates. But the data are not completely conclusive. It is almost certainly the case that a part of the additional use of cardiac procedures in the United States is due to overuse. See Mark et al., "Use of Medical Resources and Quality of Life after Acute Myocardial Infarction in Canada and the United States"; Pilote et al., "Differences in the

Treatment of Myocardial Infarction in the United States and Canada"; Rouleau et al., "A Comparison of Management Patterns after Acute Myocardial Infarction in Canada and the United States."

46. For a listing and discussion of the many papers on this topic by the Rand team, see "Assessing the Appropriateness of Care: How Much Is Too Much?" Rand Health Research Highlights (Santa Monica: Rand Corporation, 1998). Specific studies include: Steven J. Bernstein et al., "The Appropriateness of Hysterectomy: A Comparison of Care in Seven Health Plans," *Journal of the American Medical Association* 269, no.18 (May 12, 1993): 2398–2402; Mark R. Chassin et al., "How Coronary Angioplasty Is Used: Clinical Determinants of Appropriateness," *Journal of the American Medical Association* 258, no. 18 (November 13, 1987): 2543–47; Lawrence C. Kleinman et al., "The Medical Appropriateness of Tympanostomy Tubes Proposed for Children Younger than 16 Years in the United States," *Journal of the American Medical Association* 271, no. 16 (April 27, 1994): 1250–55; Constance M. Winslow et al., "The Appropriateness of Performing Coronary Artery Bypass Surgery," *Journal of the American Medical Association* 260, no. 4 (July 22–29, 1988): 505–9; Constance M. Winslow et al., "The Appropriateness of Carotid Endarterectomy," *New England Journal of Medicine* 318, no. 12 (March 24, 1988): 721–27.

47. American College of Cardiology and American Hospital Association, "ACC/AHA Guidelines and Indications for Coronary Artery Bypass Graft: A Report of the American College of Cardiology/American Heart Association Task Force on Assessment of Diagnostic and Therapeutic Cardiovascular Procedures, Subcommittee on Coronary Artery Bypass Surgery, "*Circulation* 83, no. 3 (March 1991): 1125–73. For data on California hospitals, see Cheryl L. Damberg, Robert E. Chung, and Anthony Steimle, *The California Report on Coronary Artery Bypass Graft Surgery: 1997–1998 Hospital Data, Summary Report* (San Francisco: Pacific Business Group on Health and the California Office of Statewide Health Planning and Development, July 2001). This is a major difference between the United States and Canada. In Canada, where very few hospitals are allowed to perform bypass surgery, the vast majority of patients are treated at high-volume institutions. See Kevin Grumbach et al., "Regionalization of Cardiac Surgery in the United States and Canada: Geographic Access, Choice, and Outcomes," *Journal of the American Medical Association* 274, no. 16 (October 25, 1995): 1282–88. This could be part of the reason that mortality after a heart attack is so similar in the United States and Canada, despite a much higher surgery rate in the United States.

48. Vicki L. Burt et al., "Trends in the Prevalence, Awareness, Treatment, and Control of Hypertension in the Adult US Population," 60–69.

49. Maureen I. Harris et al., "Racial and Ethnic Differences in Glycemic Control of Adults with Type 2 Diabetes," *Diabetes Care* 22, no. 3 (March 1999): 403–8; Patrick McBride et al., "Primary Care Practice Adherence to National Cholesterol Education Program Guidelines for Patients with Coronary Heart Disease," *Archives of Internal Medicine* 158, no. 11 (June 8, 1998): 1238–44.

6 Medical Care: Of What Value

1. Premium data are in Kaiser Family Foundation and Health Research and Educational Trust, *Employer Health Benefits, 2002 Annual Survey* (Washington, D.C.: Kaiser Family Foundation, 2002). Even if the employer nominally pays the bill for some of the policy, the employer is likely to offset the health insurance costs with lower wages One way or another, the worker will pay the cost.

2. Kevin Rask and Kimberly Rask, "Public Insurance Substituting for Private Insurance: New Evidence Regarding Public Hospitals, Uncompensated Care Funds, and Medicaid," *Journal of Health Economics* 19, no. 1 (January 2000): 1–31; Bradley Herring, "Does Access to Charity Care for the Uninsured Crowd Out Private Health Insurance Coverage?" unpublished manuscript.

3. Most of the decline in insurance coverage in the 1990s was not among people whose employers stopped offering coverage. Rather, it was among workers who increasingly turned down insurance when offered. See David M. Cutler, "Employee Costs and the Decline in Health Insurance Coverage," in *Frontiers in Health Policy Research,* vol. 6, ed. David M. Cutler and Alan Garber (Cambridge: MIT Press, 2003); Michael Chernew, David Cutler, and Patricia Keenan, "Rising Health Care Costs and the Decline in Insurance Coverage," unpublished manuscript.

4. Institute of Medicine, *Care Without Coverage: Too Little, Too Late* (Washington, D.C.: National Academy Press, 2002).

5. For the specific example of breast cancer, see John Z. Ayanian et al., "The Relation between Health Insurance Coverage and Clinical Outcomes among Women with Breast Cancer," *New England Journal of Medicine* 329, no. 5 (July 29, 1993): 326–31; Richard G. Roetzheim et al., "Effects of Health Insurance and Race on Early Detection of Cancer," *Journal of the National Cancer Institute* 91, no. 16 (August 18, 1999): 1409–15; Richard G. Roetzheim et al., "Effects of Health Insurance and Race on Breast Carcinoma Treatments and Outcomes," *Cancer* 89, no. 11 (December 1, 2000): 2202–13; and Anna Lee-Feldstein et al., "The Relationship of HMOs, Health Insurance, and Delivery Systems to Breast Cancer Outcomes," *Medical Care* 38, no. 7 (July 2000): 705–18.

6. These deaths are among adults aged 25–64, as are the subsequent calculations.

7. For estimates of these costs, see Susan Marquis and Stephen H. Long, "The Uninsured Access Gap: Narrowing the Estimates," *Inquiry* 31 (Winter 1994/5): 405–14. A common hope is that if the uninsured had insurance, the improvement in their health would be sufficiently great that they would spend less on medical care. That might be true down the road, but it is not true in the near term. For the foreseeable future, insuring the uninsured would add to total medical spending.

8. Center for Evaluative Clinical Sciences, *Dartmouth Atlas of Health Care* (Chicago: American Hospital Association, 2000).

9. Jonathan Skinner and Jack Wennberg, "The Efficiency of Medicare," unpublished manuscript.

10. David W. Bates et al., "Effect of Computerized Physician Order Entry and a Team Intervention on Prevention of Serious Medication Errors," *Journal of the American Medical Association* 280, no. 15 (October 21, 1998): 1311–16. In one large hospital, for example, a computerized drug order entry system cut the rate of medication errors in half.

11. Institute of Medicine, *To Err is Human: Building a Safer Health System* (Washington, D.C.: National Academy Press, 1999). The mortality estimate has generated some controversy. See Clement J. McDonald, Michael Weiner, and Siu L. Hui, "Deaths Due to Medical Errors Are Exaggerated in Institute of Medicine Report," *Journal of the American Medical Association* 284, no. 1 (July 5, 2000): 93–95, and the reply by Lucien Leape, "Institute of Medicine Medical Error Figures Are Not Exaggerated," *Journal of the American Medical Association* 284, no. 1 (July 5, 2000): 95–97.

12. A recent study estimates that only 55 percent of recommended care was received. Elizabeth A. McGlynn, et al., "The Quality of Health Care Delivered to Adults in the United States" *New England Jorurnal of Medicine* 348, no. 26 (June 26, 2003): 2635–45.

13. Evidence on the survival benefits of beta-blockers is presented in Harlan M. Krumholz et al., "National Use and Effectiveness of Beta-Blockers for the Treatment of Elderly Patients after Acute Myocardial Infarction," *Journal of the American Medical Association* 280, no. 7 (August 19, 1998): 623–29; Salim Yusuf, Janet Wittes, and Lawrence Friedman, "Overview of Results of Randomized Clinical Trials in Heart Disease I: Treatments Following Myocardial Infarction," *Journal of the American Medical Association* 260, no. 14 (October 14, 1988): 2088–93. Beta-blockers cost about a dollar a day per patient. Many researchers suggest the true costs are smaller, however, because people on beta-blockers have fewer recurrent heart attacks and thus spend less on future heart attacks. Cost-effectiveness analysis is presented in Kathryn A. Phillips et al., "Health and Economic Benefits of Increased Beta-Blocker Use Following Myocardial Infarction," *Journal of the American Medical Association* 284, no. 21 (December 6, 2000): 2748–54.

14. Edward F. Ellerbeck et al., "Quality of Care for Medicare Patients with Acute Myocardial Infarction: A Four-State Pilot Study from the Cooperative Cardiovascular Project," *Journal of the American Medical Association* 273, no. 19 (May 17, 1995): 1509–14; Thomas J. McLaughlin et al., "Adherence to National Guidelines for Drug Treatment of Suspected Acute Myocardial Infarction: Evidence for Undertreatment in Women and the Elderly," *Archives of Internal Medicine* 156, no. 7 (April 8, 1996): 799–805; Harlan M. Krumholz et al., "National Use and Effectiveness of β-Blockers for the Treatment of Elderly Patients after Acute Myocardial Infarction: National Cooperative Cardiovascular Project," *Journal of the American Medical Association* 280, no. 7 (August 19, 1998): 623–29; Stephen F. Jencks et al., "Quality of Medical Care Delivered to Medicare Beneficiaries: A Profile at State and National Levels," *Journal of the American Medical Association* 284, no. 13 (October 4, 2000): 1670–76.

15. Stephen B. Soumerai et al., "Adverse Outcomes of Underuse of Beta-Blockers in Elderly Survivors of Acute Myocardial Infarction," *Journal of the American Medical Association* 277, no. 2 (January 8, 1997): 115–21.

16. Paula A. Rochon et al., "Use of Beta-Blocker Therapy in Older Patients after Acute Myocardial Infarction in Ontario," *Canadian Medical Association Journal* 161, no. 11 (November 30, 1999): 1403–8; Louise Pilote et al., "Changes in the Treatment and Outcomes of Acute Myocardial Infarction in Quebec, 1988–1995," *Canadian Medical Association Journal* 163, no. 1 (July 11, 2000): 31–36; Antonia Agusti, Josep Maria Arnau, and Joan-Ramon Laporte, "Clinical Trials Versus Clinical Practice in the Secondary Prevention of Myocardial Infarction," *European Journal of Clinical Pharmacology* 46, no. 2 (1994): 95–99.

17. John Z. Ayanian et al., "Knowledge and Practices of Generalist and Specialist Physicians Regarding Drug Therapy for Acute Myocardial Infarction," *New England Journal of Medicine* 331, no. 17 (October 27, 1994): 1136–42.

18. Mark R. Chassin, "Is Health Care Ready for Six Sigma Quality?" *Milbank Quarterly* 76, no. 4 (December 1998): 565–91.

19. David Wessel, "The Magic Elixir of Productivity," *Wall Street Journal*, February 15, 2001, p. A1.

20. David Cutler and Mark McClellan, "Is Technological Change in Medical Care Worth It?" *Health Affairs* 20, no. 5 (September/October 2001): 11–29; David Cutler and Robert Huckman, "Technological Development and Medical Productivity: The Diffusion of Angioplasty in New York State," *Journal of Health Economics* 22, no. 2 (March 2003): 187–217.

21. Richard D. Lamm, "A New Moral Vision for Health Care," unpublished manuscript.

22. For a general discussion, see William B. Schwartz, *Life Without Disease: The Pursuit of Medical Utopia* (Berkeley and Los Angeles: University of California Press, 1998). In addition, there is an excellent issue of the

Journal of the American Medical Association 285, no. 5 (February 7, 2001) devoted to opportunities for medical research in the twenty-first century. Some of the specific articles are cited below.

23. Francis S. Collins and Victor A. McKusick, "Implications of the Human Genome Project for Medical Science," *Journal of the American Medical Association* 285, no. 5 (February 7, 2001): 540–44; Francis S. Collins, "Shattuck Lecture—Medical and Societal Consequences of the Human Genome Project," *New England Journal of Medicine* 341, no. 1 (July 1, 1999): 28–37.

24. Eugene H. Kaji and Jeffrey M. Leiden, "Gene and Stem Cell Therapies," *Journal of the American Medical Association* 285, no. 5 (February 7, 2001): 545–50.

25. Michael Chernew, Richard Hirth, and David Cutler, "Paying for Rising Health Care Costs: How Much Health Care Spending Can We Afford?" unpublished manuscript.

26. Technical Review Panel on the Medicare Trustees' Reports, "Review of Assumptions and Methods of the Medicare Trustees' Financial Projections" (Washington, D.C.: Government Printing Office, 2000).

7 You Get What You Pay For

1. Paul Starr, *The Social Transformation of American Medicine* (New York: Basic Books, 1982).

2. Melissa A. Thomasson, "The Importance of Group Coverage: How Tax Policy Shaped US Health Insurance," *American Economic Review* (2003).

3. Jon Gabel et al., "Job Based Health Insurance in 2000: Premiums Rise Sharply While Coverage Grows," *Health Affairs* 19, no. 5 (September/ October 2000): 144–51.

4. Adam Smith, *An Inquiry into the Nature and the Causes of the Wealth of Nations*, ed. E. Cannon (New York: Modern Library, 1937).

5. George Bernard Shaw, *The Doctors Dilemma* (New York: Brentano's, 1911).

6. This became known as "usual, customary, and reasonable" fees.

7. Joseph DiMasi et al., "The Cost of Innovation in the Pharmaceutical Industry," *Journal of Health Economics* 10, no. 2 (July 1991): 107–42.

8. Michael Kremer, "Creating Markets for New Vaccines, Part I: Rationale," and "Part II: Design", in Adam B. Jaffe, Josh Lerner, and Scott Stern, eds., *Innovation Policy and the Economy* (Cambridge, MA: MIT Press, 2001).

8 The Managed Care Debacle

1. The beginnings of this trend occurred before managed care. The federal government moved from a fee-for-service payment system for

hospitals to admission-based payment in the mid-1980s. Additional care provided during the inpatient stay is not reimbursed at higher rates. But managed care has taken this idea much further.

2. David Cutler, Mark McClellan, and Joseph Newhouse, "How Does Managed Care Do It?" *Rand Journal of Economics* 31, no. 3 (Autumn 2000): 526–48.

3. Of course, paying less for doctors may lead to fewer people entering into medicine over time, or to the best people not entering the field. But these long-term effects are not of much concern to managed care insurers and employers focused on short-run savings.

4. Prescription drug cost sharing has increased recently, but it, too, is below traditional insurance levels.

5. For a summary, see Sherry Glied, "Managed Care," in *Handbook of Health Economics,* ed. Anthony Culyer and Joseph Newhouse (Amsterdam: Elsevier, 2000).

6. Roland Sturm and Kenneth Wells, *Caring for Depression* (Cambridge: Harvard University Press, 1996).

7. Mark J. Sada et al., "Influence of Payor on Use of Invasive Cardiac Procedures and Patient Outcomes after Myocardial Infarction in the United States," *Journal of the American College of Cardiology* 31, no. 7 (June 1998): 1474–80; Eduard Guadagnoli et al., "Appropriateness of Coronary Angiography after Myocardial Infarction in Medicare Beneficiaries: Managed Care versus Fee for Service," *New England Journal of Medicine* 343, no. 20 (November 16, 2000): 1460–66.

8. Cutler, McClellan, and Newhouse, "How Does Managed Care Do It?" 526–48.

9. For a summary of the literature through November 1995, see Joshua J. Seidman, Eric P. Bass, and Haya R. Rubin, "Review of Studies That Compare the Quality of Cardiovascular Care in HMO Versus Non-HMO Settings," *Medical Care* 36, no. 12 (December 1998): 1607–25. See also Steven B. Soumerai et al., "Timeliness and Quality of Care for Elderly Patients with Acute Myocardial Infarction under Health Maintenance Organization vs. Fee-for-Service Insurance," *Archives of Internal Medicine* 159, no. 17 (September 27, 1999): 2013–20.

10. Mark J. Sada et al., "Influence of Payor on Use of Invasive Cardiac Procedures and Patient Outcomes after Myocardial Infarction in the United States," 1474–80; and Cutler, McClellan, and Newhouse, "How Does Managed Care Do It?" 526–48.

11. Robert H. Miller and Harold S. Luft, "Does Managed Care Lead to Better or Worse Quality of Care?" *Health Affairs* 16, no. 5 (September/October 1997): 7–25.

12. David Cutler and Louise Sheiner, "Managed Care and the Growth of Medical Expenditures," in *Frontiers in Health Policy Research,* vol. 1, ed.

Alan Garber (Cambridge: MIT Press, 1998), 77–116; Laurence C. Baker and Susan K. Wheeler, "Managed Care and Technology Diffusion: The Case of MRI," *Health Affairs* 17, no. 5 (September/October 1998): 195–207; Laurence C. Baker and Joanne Spetz, "Managed Care and Medical Technology Growth" in *Frontiers in Health Policy Research*, vol. 2, ed. Alan Garber (Cambridge: MIT Press, 1999), 27–52; Laurence C. Baker, "Managed Care, Technology Adoption, and Health Care: The Adoption of Neonatal Intensive Care," *Rand Journal of Economics* 33, no. 3 (Autumn 2002): 524–48; Laurence C. Baker, "Managed Care and Technology Adoption: Evidence from Magnetic Resonance Imaging," *Journal of Health Economics* 20, no. 3 (May 2001): 395–421; Michael E. Chernew et al., "Managed Care, Medical Technology, and Health Care Cost Growth: A Review of the Evidence," *Medical Care Research and Review* 55, no. 3 (September 1998): 259–88.

13. Laurence C. Baker and Martin L. Brown, "The Effect of Managed Care on Medical Care Providers," *Rand Journal of Economics* 30, no. 2 (Summer 1999): 351–74; Laurence C. Baker, "Association of Managed Care Market Share and Health Expenditures for Fee-for-Service Medicare Patients," *Journal of the American Medical Association* 281, no. 5 (February 3, 1999): 432–37.

14. Paul A. Heidenreich et al., "The Relations between Managed Care Market Share and the Treatment of Elderly Fee-for-Service Patients with Myocardial Infarction," *American Journal of Medicine* 112, no. 3 (February 15, 2002): 176–82.

15. Mark J. Sada et al., "Influence of Payor on Use of Invasive Cardiac Procedures and Patient Outcomes after Myocardial Infarction in the United States"; Heidenreich et al., "The Relation between Managed Care Market Share and the Treatment of Elderly Fee-for-Service Patients with Myocardial Infarction."

16. Robert Blendon et al., "Understanding the Managed Care Backlash," *Health Affairs* 17, no. 4 (July/August 1998): 80–94.

17. Statement of Senator Edward M. Kennedy on managed care, Office of Senator Edward M. Kennedy, July 8, 1998.

18. Nancy Beaulieu, "Externalities in Overlapping Supplier Networks," unpublished manuscript, 2002.

19. A related phenomenon is that providing high-quality care encourages sick people, who then spend more in future years, to stay in the plan. In work with colleagues of mine, I have termed this adverse retention. See Daniel Altman, David Cutler, and Richard Zeckhauser, "Adverse Selection and Adverse Retention," *American Economic Review* 88, no. 2 (May 1998): 122–26.

9 Paying for Health

1. Nancy Beaulieu, David Cutler, and Katherine Ho, "The Business Case for Disease Management at Two Managed Care Organizations: A Case Study of Diabetes Management at Health Partners and Independent Health Association," unpublished manuscript, 2003.

2. Literally hundreds of studies in the medical literature have examined the impact of better self-management systems for care of chronic disease. Most studies find that they have strong positive effects. See Center for the Advancement of Health, *Indexed Bibliography of Behavioral Interventions of Chronic Disease* (Washington, D.C.: Center for the Advancement of Health, 1996); Edward H. Wagner, Brian T. Austin, and Michael von Korff, "Organizing Care for Patients with Chronic Illness," *Milbank Quarterly* 74, no. 4 (December 1996): 511–44. For evidence of specific diabetes programs, see Ronald E. Aubert et al., "Nurse Case Management to Improve Glycemic Control in Diabetic Patients in a Health Maintenance Organization: A Randomized, Controlled Trial," *Annals of Internal Medicine* 129, no. 8 (October 15, 1998): 605–12; and Robert J. Rubin, Kimberly A. Dietrich, and Anne D. Hawk, "Clinical and Economic Impact of Implementing a Comprehensive Diabetes Management Program in Managed Care," *Journal of Clinical Endocrinology and Metabolism* 83, no. 8 (August 1998): 2635–42.

3. See, for example, New York State Department of Health, *Coronary Artery Bypass Surgery in New York State, 1996–1998* (Albany: New York State Department of Health, 2001).

4. Mark R. Chassin, Edward L. Hannan, and Barbara A. DeBuono, "Benefits and Hazards of Reporting Medical Outcomes Publicly, *New England Journal of Medicine* 334, no. 6 (February 8, 1996): 394–98; Edward L. Hannan et al., "Improving the Quality of Coronary Artery Bypass Surgery in New York State," *Journal of the American Medical Association* 271, no. 1 (March 9, 1994): 761–66.

5. There is debate about whether or not the system was really effective. Arguments that very sick patients are being operated on less frequently are found in Nbowamagbe A. Omoigui et al., "Outmigration for Coronary Bypass Surgery in an Era of Public Dissemination of Clinical Outcomes," *Circulation* 93, no. 1 (January 1, 1996): 27–33; and in David Dranove et al., "Is More Information Better? The Effects of Health Care 'Report Cards,' " *Journal of Political Economy* 111, no. 3 (June 2003): 555–88. Dissenting evidence is cited in Chassin, Hannan, and DeBuono, "Benefits and Hazards of Reporting Medical Outcomes Publicly."

6. National Center for Quality Assurance, *The State of Managed Care* (Washington, D.C.: National Center for Quality Assurance, 2001).

7. A group of large employers in California has worked with managed care

companies in that state for nearly a decade to measure and improve quality. The group specifies certain performance measures and negotiates targets with each plan. There is some financial payment for plans meeting the quality goals, although the payments are not extremely large. Still, the system is widely viewed as a partial success. See Helen Halpin Schauffler and Tracy Rodriguez, "Exercising Purchasing Power for Preventive Care," *Health Affairs* 15, no. 1 (Spring 1996): 73–85; and Helen Halpin Schauffler, Catherine Brown, and Arnold Milstein, "Raising the Bar: The Use of Performance Guarantees by the Pacific Business Group on Health," *Health Affairs* 18, no. 2 (March/April 1999): 134–42.

8. In the early 1990s, many large employers in Minneapolis came together and pushed for a system of quality accountability in medical care. They called themselves the Business Health Care Action Group. Best practices were going to be identified, and employers would only contract with providers meeting these best practices. Overall quality of care would improve. Alas, the theory was never completely realized. The business group in Minnesota has deteriorated, although its effects linger in programs like that which publishes clinical standards. See Jon Christianson et al., "Early Experience with a New Model of Employer Group Purchasing in Minnesota," *Health Affairs* 18, no. 6 (November/December 1999): 100–14.

9. Amendments to the Clean Air Act were passed in 1977. For purposes of this discussion, I consider the original legislation and amendments together, since they were operationally very similar.

10. The results presented here, along with the regulatory history, are largely based on the work by A. Denny Ellerman et al., *Markets for Clean Air: The U.S. Acid Rain Program* (Cambridge: Cambridge University Press, 2000). That book refers to other research papers of note.

11. The Agency for Health Care Research and Quality, for example, has developed a survey titled the Consumer Assessment of Health Plans, or CAHPS.

12. There is a theoretical basis for determining how strong these payment incentives should be. One can think of paying for health as correcting the barriers to quality improvement noted in the last chapter. An insurer that implements a quality-improvement program does not capture all the benefits. The magnitude of the discrepancy between the social benefits and the benefits to the insurer tells how large the bonus should be. In practice, the exact magnitude of this discrepancy is not known, so the appropriate bonus is a matter of some guesswork.

13. Frank Sloan and Bruce Steinwald, "Regulatory Approaches to Hospital Cost Containment: A Synthesis of the Empirical Evidence," in *A New Approach to the Economics of Health Care*, ed. Mancur Olsen (Washington, D.C.: American Enterprise Institute, 1981), 274–308.

10 Universal Benefits

1. This is termed the Federal Employees Health Benefits Program.

2. This statistic is from the March 2001 Current Population Survey, as tabulated by the Census Department.

3. For discussion, see the *Covering America* series from the Economic and Social Research Institute in Washington, D.C.

4. One might wonder why universal coverage is needed if everyone can afford coverage but some choose not to buy it. There are two reasons. First, some people do not have an accurate knowledge of their risks. People who are generally healthy may not perceive a need for insurance coverage, even though some will have an unforeseen need for care (a 25-year-old motorcycle rider who has an accident, for example). Second, even those with knowledge of risks may decide not to purchase coverage because they know that charity care will pay for them should they need services. This "crowding out"—inducing people not to buy what they otherwise value—imposes a burden on everyone else that mandatory insurance coverage would prevent.

5. For illustrative purposes, I have considered a proposal that offers a subsidy of $2,500 for individuals and $7,000 for families below the poverty line. The subsidy declines to $500 per family for all families earning 250 percent of the poverty line or higher. The non-elderly, non-disabled Medicaid population is included in the subsidized population, and the funds from the existing Medicaid program are directed to the subsidy pool. The net cost is about $120 billion per year.

6. These data are from the Urban-Brookings Tax Policy Center Microsimulation Model and refer to the legislation if the sunsets were removed, as the Bush Administration wants; see www.taxpolicycenter.org.

7. According to official estimates, the tax cut passed in 2001 has a revenue cost of $187 billion per year in 2010, well above what is required for universal insurance coverage. The 2003 tax cut has a revenue cost of $17 billion in 2008, before many provisions sunset.

8. See David Himmelstein and Steffie Woolhandler et al., "A National Health Program for the United States: A Physicians' Proposal," *New England Journal of Medicine* 320, no. 2 (January 12, 1989): 102–8.

9. Administrative costs include many expenses. Some of the administrative expenses in the current system are clearly wasteful. Examples include money spent screening out high-cost people, and resources that physicians spend dealing with multiple payment systems. Other administrative savings may be valuable. Money spent eliminating overused care, if used right, saves total resources without adverse health outcomes. There has been a lot of discussion about whether Canada's medical system is more efficient than the U.S. system, because of its reduced administrative expenses. Money spent on administrative services is smaller in Canada

than in the United States, but waits and other uncounted spending offset some of these monetary savings. For a summary of the debate, see Steffie Woolhandler and David U. Himmelstein, "The Deteriorating Administrative Efficiency of the U.S. Health Care System," *New England Journal of Medicine* 324, no. 18 (May 2, 1991): 1253–58; Steffie Woolhandler and David U. Himmelstein, "Costs of Care and Administration at For-Profit and other Hospitals in the United States," *New England Journal of Medicine* 336, no. 11, (March 13, 1997): 769–74; Patricia Danzon, "Hidden Overhead Costs: Is Canada's System Really Less Expensive?" *Health Affairs* 11, no. 1, (Spring 1992): 21–40; and Stuart H. Altman and David Shactman, "Should We Worry About Hospitals' High Administrative Costs?" *New England Journal of Medicine* 336, no. 11 (March 13, 1997): 798–99.

10. The strongest proponent of this approach is the AFL-CIO.

Acknowledgments

A number of people helped immensely in the shaping of this book. Special thanks are due to my coauthors whose work is reported here: Nancy Beaulieu, Kate Ho, Srikanth Kadiyala, Mark McClellan, Ellen Meara, Joe Newhouse, Dahlia Remler, and Elizabeth Richardson Vigdor. I owe special thanks to Ernst Berndt, Susan Busch, and Richard Frank for providing me with data tabulations used in the chapter on mental illness. It is rare and gratifying to find researchers as generous as they are. In addition to those mentioned above, a number of people have offered comments on all or several parts of the book, or have spent time talking about the ideas with me. I am grateful to all of them: Henry Aaron, Michael Aaronson, Philip Aspden, Jason Barro, Nicholas Christakis, Jonathan Cohen, Andrew Cutler, Jennifer Cutler, Angus Deaton, Mihir Desai, Rashi Fein, Martin Feldstein, Alan Garber, Ed Glaeser, Sherry Glied, Claudia Goldin, Jonathan Gruber, Jill Horwitz, Alexandra Houck, Robert Huckman, Steve Hyman, Chad Jones, Larry Katz, Dan Kessler, Bill Kirby, Mary Beth Landrum, Jeffrey Liebman, Tom McGuire, Barbara McNeil, Ted Parsons, Christina Paxson, Jim Poterba, Sarah Reber, John Rosenberg, Michael Rothschild, Walter Shalick, Andrei Shleifer, Roland Sturm, Larry Summers, Richard Suzman, Carla Vaccaro, David Weil, and Richard Zeckhauser. Special thanks also to my agent Barbara Rifkind, and my terrific editor, Tim Bartlett.

The research reported here was sponsored by several sources. The National Institutes of Health has been particularly interested in these topics; this project could not have been undertaken without its support. The National Bureau of Economic Research has provided a wonderful home for the research and has been a great source of feedback. Key financial support was also provided by the Commonwealth Foundation, the Russell Sage Foundation, and the Robert Wood Johnson Foundation. Some of this work was conducted while I was a fellow at the Center for Advanced Study in Behavioral Sciences. I am very grateful for their wonderful gift of leave.

In the end, none of these individuals or organizations bears any responsibility for what is reported here. The good, and the bad, are entirely mine.

Index